Mark Twain:

His Life In Virginia City, Nevada

George Williams III

Tree By The River Publishing
P.O. Box 935 VC
Dayton, Nevada 89403

Mark Twain: His Life in Virginia City, Nevada
by George J. Williams III

Published by:
Tree By The River Publishing
P.O. Box 935-MTVC
Dayton, Nevada 89403

To order books with Visa or MastCard or to request a free brochure of the author's books call 1-800-487-6610, 9 AM to 5 PM West Coast time Monday through Friday.

Other related non-fiction books by George Williams III:
  Mark Twain: His Life In Virginia City, Nevada *(1986)*
  Mark Twain: His Adventures at Aurora and Mono Lake *(1987)*
  Mark Twain: Jackass Hill and the Jumping Frog *(1988)*
  On the Road with Mark Twain in California and Nevada *(1993)*
  Rosa May: The Search for a Mining Camp Legend *(1979)*
  The Redlight Ladies of Virginia City, Nevada *(1984)*
  The Guide to Bodie and Eastern Sierra Historic Sites *(1982)*
  The Murders at Convict Lake *(1984)*
  The Songwriter's Demo Manual and Success Guide *(1984)*
  Hot Springs of the Eastern Sierra *(1988)*
  In The Last of the Wild West *(1992)*

Library of Congress Cataloging-in-Publication Data
Williams, George, III, 1949-
  Mark Twain: his life in Virginia City, Nevada
1. Twain, Mark, 1835-1910—Homes and haunts—Nevada—Virginia City 2. Virginia City (Nev)—History 3. Authors, American—19th century—Biography. 4. Journalism—Nevada—Virginia City—History. 5. Daily Territorial Enterprise (Virginia City, Nev.)
I. Title
PS1334.W55 1985 818'.409 85-16483
ISBN 0-935174-16-8
ISBN 0-935174-15-X (pbk.)

Printed in the United States of America

For my mother, Millie Williams
who gave me life,
And for my father, George Williams, Jr.,
who taught me right from wrong.

Table of Contents

AUTHOR'S INTRODUCTION

It was in Virginia City, Nevada, a silver mining town 15 miles northeast of Carson City, where Sam Clemens first conjured his now world famous pen name, Mark Twain. Though Twain is usually associated with the Mississippi River, *Tom Sawyer* and *Huckleberry Finn*, Twain spent a little over five years in Nevada and California where he lived wildly, became a silver miner and discovered his life's work while writing for the *Territorial Enterprise* newspaper at Virginia City. Some beleive if Sam Clemens had not ventured to Nevada, he would not have become the great author and humorist we know as Mark Twain.

This is more or less a biography of Mark Twain from July, 1861 to May, 1864, between the ages of twenty-five and twenty-eight. This book tells why Clemens came to Nevada, briefly covers his time as a silver miner and concentrates on Mark Twain's reporting career for the *Enterprise*. Though primarily written for the general reader, Twain students will find much useful information here.

In wild and free living Virginia City, Mark Twain met and became friends with men of extraordinary talents. These men tremendously influenced Twain's development as a writer and as a person. Most remained Mark Twain's friends their entire lives. Some advised him with important career decisions. Nearly all went on to become successful in their individual fields. Much information about these men and their relationship to Mark Twain is included here. Great efforts went into uncovering photographs of Mark Twain's Nevada friends. Some photographs included here have not been published.

Some of the places where Mark Twain lived, worked and played still exist today in Nevada. I have photographed existing historic sites,and have provided road directions for those who wish to retrace Mark Twain's life in Nevada as I have done. A detailed map is included to help travelers in this pursuit.

Much has been written about Twain's Nevada years and there is abundant material available for those who seek it. I have endeavored to rely on what I consider primary sources. These are the letters Mark Twain wrote to relatives and friends while living in Nevada and afterward, journals and recollections of men who worked with or knew Twain and local and regional newspaper articles.

Secondary sources are Twain's published writings, primarily,

Roughing It and *The Autobiography of Mark Twain*, which are at times unreliable due to Twain's wonderful imagination and his need to exaggerate. Though many books and articles about Twain were consulted, I have based the heart of this book on the above primary and secondary sources and my own field work while living in Virginia City and Carson City.

Personally, I have a special affinity for Mark Twain's years in the mining towns of the eastern Sierra and norhtwestern Nevada. These mining towns are places I have lived in or visited often, and whose histories I have written about for more than ten years. My career as professional writer and publisher began in this region at about the same age Mark Twain decided on writing as a career. Even before I developed an interest in Twain's Western years, I visited and wrote about Aurora where Clemens was a silver miner, swam in Mono Lake where he nearly lost his life and drank in a Virginia City saloon where more than a hundred years earlier Mark Twain and fellow "Companions of the Jug" used to drink. Hopefully this backyard knowledge of the region, its mining, geography, customs, and history, will have aided in accurately sketching Mark Twain's life in Virginia City.

Most aspiring writers enjoy reading about successful writers. In their lives and careers, the aspiring writer may find seeds for his own success. Before he was successful, Mark Twain was a struggling unknown in an isolated region of America. Yet he had an uncanny way of manipulating situations for his benefit. Perhaps these many years later, aspiring writers and others will find in Mark Twain's early career ways to achieve their own success.

This is the first in a series of five books I have written about Mark Twain's Western years. Other books in this series which cover specific periods of his Western career are, MARK TWAIN: HIS ADVENTURES AT AURORA AND MONO LAKE, MARK TWAIN: JACKASS HILL AND THE JUMPING FROG, ON THE ROAD WITH MARK TWAIN IN NEVADA and MARK TWAIN IN SAN FRANCISCO. Readers may find these books in their library, at their local book store or you may order autographed copies directly from the publisher by using the order form at the end of this book.

I thoroughly enjoyed researching and writing this book and I hope you enjoy reading it. Here's to Mark Twain, one of the funniest writers I have ever read.

In a race, everyone runs but only one person gets first prize. So run your race to win. To win the contest you must deny yourselves many things that would keep you from doing your best. An athlete goes to all this trouble just to win a blue ribbon or a silver cup, but we do it for a heavenly reward that never disappears. So I run straight to the goal with purpose in every step. I fight to win. I'm not just shadow-boxing or playing around. Like an athlete I punish my body, treating it roughly, training it to do what it should, not what it wants to. Otherwise I fear that after enlisting others for the race, I myself might be declared unfit and ordered to stand aside.

Paul, the Apostle, *1 Corinthians 9:24-27*

Necessity is the mother of "taking chances."

Mark Twain, *Roughing It*

Mark Twain as he looked at the time he worked for the *Territorial Enterprise.* **Photo taken in San Francisco,** *Mark Twain Project, Bancroft Library.*

CHAPTER ONE

Sam Clemens Comes to Nevada

In mid-September, 1862, twenty-six year old Sam Clemens shuffled into the *Territorial Enterprise* offices in Virginia City, Nevada. Rollin M. Daggett who was there when Clemens first walked in, recalled that Clemens looked like he "had been living on alkali water and whang leather, with only a sufficient supply of the former for drinking purposes, for several months, and you may imagine his appearance when I first saw him." Clemens had a beard half down to his waist. He was wearing a blue wool miner's shirt and worn pants stuffed into his work boots. Slung around his waist was a navy revolver and holster which Clemens got rid of once he had acquired a "more Christian attire." Clemens admitted he had no use for the gun anyway and only wore it because everyone else did.

Sam Clemens was a broke silver miner at Aurora when Joe Goodman, editor and co-owner of the *Enterprise* offered him a job as a local reporter at $25 a week. Clemens had been prospecting at Aurora four months when Goodman's offer arrived in late July, 1862. Though Clemens accepted the job, he remained in Aurora until mid-September. His mining claims, though at times promising, never paid off.

Clemens was in Nevada about fourteen months before he settled in Virginia City. He went to Nevada with his older brother Orion, who had recently been appointed Secretary of Nevada Territory by Ed Bates, an old friend and a member of Lincoln's cabinet. Sam went West with Orion for a combination of reasons.

For four and a half years, Clemens had been a river pilot on the Mississippi. The outbreak of the Civil War closed the river. Sam lost his high paying job-$250 a month, an extraordinary income at that time.

Secondly, Clemens wanted no part of the Civil War. Though he joined the Marion Rangers, a Confederate militia in Hannibal, Missouri, Clemens left after a month. Before leaving for Nevada he told his niece, Annie Moffett, he feared he would be arrested by government agents and forced to pilot military gun boats. Clemens avoided soldiers before leaving for Nevada.

Last, Clemens had long been infatuated with the West. He had heard stories since boyhood of men who went West and made their fortunes in the gold mines. Clemens was aware Orion would be stationed at Carson City, only fifteen miles from Virginia City whose incredible silver mines had attracted national attention. As a river pilot, Clemens had tasted the good life and he liked it. He had become accustomed to having plenty of money, wearing the best clothes and eating in the finest restaurants. Clemens desired not only to maintain this level of living, he wanted to become rich. Highly intuitive, he may have sensed good fortune awaited him in Nevada Territory.

The loss of his river piloting job, the fear of conscription, the lure of Western riches and Orion's timely appointment, led Clemens to his decision to go West.

Sam and Orion pledged to unite their energies toward one goal: to get rich in Nevada Territory. As a down payment, Sam paid $300 for he and Orion's Overland Stage tickets. On July 26, 1861, Sam and Orion left St. Joseph, Missouri for Carson City where they arrived August 14.

Sam was at first disappointed with the dust and barren landscape of Nevada. But his opinion of the Territory changed when he learned how rich it was in gold, silver, gypsum and other minerals. He wrote his mother shortly after he arrived:

Some people are malicious enough to think that if the devil were set at liberty and told to confine himself to Nevada Territory, that he would come here and look sadly around, awhile, and then get homesick and go back to hell again. But I hardly believe it, you know...Margaret wouldn't like the country, perhaps--nor the devil either, for that matter--or any other man--but I like it.

Feb. 8, 1862

Orion Clemens, Sams older brother, whose appointment as Secretary of Nevada Territory led Sam to go west. *Nevada Historical Society.*

In the Territory only a few weeks, Sam scouted for the opportunity that would make he and Orion rich. Sam and a friend hiked to Lake Tahoe where they claimed 300 acres of timber. But when their makeshift "house" which held their claim burned down along with a considerable portion of the forest, Sam returned to Carson City.

In October, with the news Aurora was the rising silver camp, Clemens made a 130 mile trip by horseback to inspect the mines. There a stranger gave him 50 feet in the "Black Warrior" mine. Clemens returned to Carson City, planning to go back to Aurora shortly.

But back in Carson City, "Humboldt! Humboldt!" became the rage, "the newest of the new, richest of the rich, the most marvelous of the marvelous discoveries in silverland..." (Roughing It). Immediately, Clemens and three friends scurried to Unionville, Humboldt Mining District, 200 miles northeast of Carson City. Clemens expected to find "masses of silver lying all over the ground glittering in the sun on the mountain summits." After a miserable two week trip in mid-December, Clemens and his friends reached Unionville, a camp of eleven cabins and a flag pole. There was "nothing doing in the district--no mining--no milling--no productive effort--no income--and not enough money in the entire camp to buy a corner lot in an eastern village..." (Roughing It). After two weeks of fruitless prospecting, Clemens left his friends and returned to Carson City in mid-January.

Clemens remained in Carson City until the first part of April, 1862, when he returned to Aurora to make a second and wholehearted attempt at silver mining. Aurora, Nevada, a silver mining camp 130 miles southeast of Carson City, in the hills north of Mono Lake, was then the latest rage.

When Clemens arrived, Aurora consisted of about 3,000 men living in canvas tents, dugouts in the hillsides, wooden shacks and out in the open. With the recent stage service from Carson City, 25-30 newcomers arrived each day. Brick buildings, a symbol of faith in a mining camp, were rapidly being thrown up. Like other mining camps, Aurora was far from a supply point. Food, feed and mining supplies were hauled 130 miles from Carson City. Food prices were high and the cost of feeding a horse for a week was astronomical.

Sam and Orion's Overland Stage receipt for their trip West. *Mark Twain Project, Bancroft Library.*

Throughout his six months at Aurora, Clemens was partners with several men, Horatio Phillips, Bob Howland, later the fearless Aurora town marshal, Cal Higbie, to whom Twain dedicated *Roughing It*, Dan Twing, and Orion.

Sam Clemens wrote nineteen letters to Orion during his stay at Aurora. A large portion of the letters are business-like filled with the latest news of claims Clemens was working or hoped to purchase. It is clear from these letters, Orion was Sam's chief business partner. Sam handled the business of investigating and buying mining claims; Orion supplied Sam with money for supplies and mine investments. Clemens apparently was partners in six claims, the Horatio and Derby, the Black Warrior, the Flyaway, the Dashaway, the Monitor and the Annipolitan. In his first letter to Orion he laid out his intentions, "I mean to make or break here within 2 or 3 months."

Clemens lived with several partners at various times in makeshift houses, with Horatio Phillips in a frame cabin, with Bob Howland in a dugout, with Cal Higbie in God knows what and with Dan Twing in a canvas tent. It snowed heavily that year through spring and into summer often preventing Clemens from prospecting and working his claims.

During his six month stay in Aurora, Clemens immersed himself in the miner's life. He learned to prospect, differentiate ores, assay, blast tunnels, mill ore and buy and trade stock. He became thoroughly familiar with the miner's hard life and simple joys. This knowledge helped him land his first full time writing job which in turn permanently changed the course of his life.

Sam and his partners scoured the hills above Aurora examining ledges and filing claims:

> We took up various claims, and commenced shafts and tunnels on them, but never finished any of them. We had to do a certain amount of work on each to "hold" it, else other parties could seize our property after the expiration of ten days. We were always hunting up new claims and doing a little work on them and waiting for a buyer--who never came. We never found any ore that would yield more than fifty dollars a ton; and as mills charged fifty dollars a ton for working the ore and extracting the silver, our pocket money soon melted away and none returned to take its place. We lived in a

little cabin and cooked for ourselves; and altogether it was a hard life, though a hopeful one--for we never ceased to expect a fortune and a customer to burst upon us someday.

Roughing It

Though Clemens was at first cautious, by May reason had taken a back seat to his emotions. He became convinced the Aurora silver mines would make he and Orion rich. In May he wrote Orion:

When you and I came out here, we did not expect '63 or '64 to find us rich men--and if that proposition had been made, we would have accepted it gladly. Now it is made...if all spare change be devoted to working the "Monitor" and "Flyaway", 12 months, or 24 at furthest, will find all our earthly wishes satisfied, so far as money is concerned...

letter to Orion, May 12, 1862

Clemens constantly wrote Orion for more money to buy and develop mining claims. Though he was often a step away from poverty, Clemens poured more money down empty holes, convinced his mining claims would one day pay off.

Life was hard but in mid-May it became violent. His Monitor claim was jumped:

Two or three of the old "Salina" company entered our hole on the Monitor yesterday morning, before our men got there, and took possession, armed with revolvers. And according to the d--d laws of this forever d--d country, nothing but the District Court (and there ain't any) can touch the matter, unless it assumes the shape of an infernal humbug which they call "forcibile entry and detainer," and in order to bring that about, you must compel the jumpers to use personal violence toward you! We went up and demanded possession, and they refused. Said they were in the hole armed and meant to die if necessary. I got in it with them, and again demanded possession. They said I might stay in it as long as I pleased, and work but they would do the same. I asked one of our company to take my place in the hole, while I went to consult a lawyer. He did so. The lawyer said it was no go. They must offer some "force."

letter to Orion, May 17, 1862

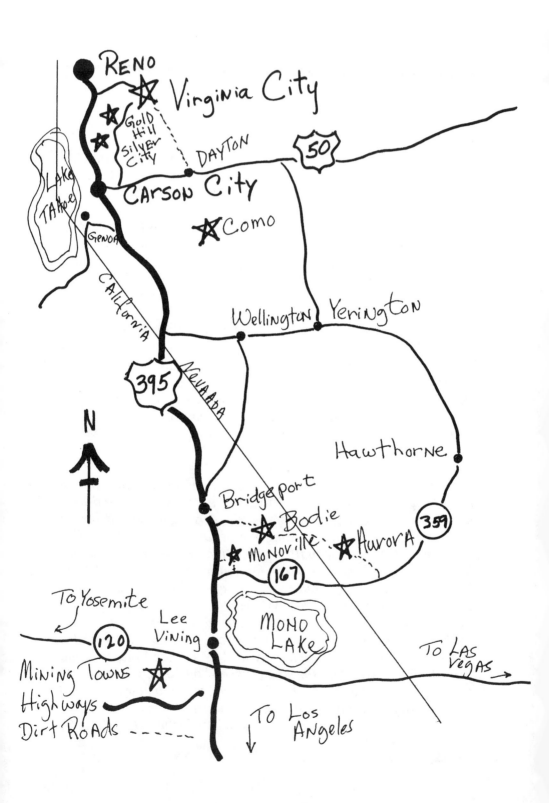

In early June, the Monitor suit was settled in court. Clemens and Phillips won though they were forced to give a portion of the Monitor to the jumpers.

In *Roughing It,* Mark Twain tells how he and Cal Higbie nearly became millionaires while involved with the Wide West mine. This was a fictionalized account based on the Monitor suit and Clemens' one promising claim: the Annipolitan.

Clemens, Phillips and Bob Howland owned the Annipolitan, a very promising claim located near the Wide West, a rich gold mine. Also located nearby were the Pride of Utah and the Dines claims. For a time the Annipolitan was believed to be a separate vein; this meant Clemens and his partners could retain ownership and work the claim. Later it was discovered the Annipolitan vein was part of the Pride of Utah. Clemens and his partners lost all rights to the Annipolitan, their best prospect.

Sam Clemens did not strike it rich at Aurora as he had hoped to. But his bitter experiences there led him to write a series of letters which won him his first important writing job.

Shortly after his arrival in Aurora, Clemens began writing humorous letters about the trials and tribulations of a hardluck miner. Clemens signed the letters "Josh" and sent them to the *Territorial Enterprise* in Virginia City where they were published. Joe Goodman was impressed by the "Josh" letters and believed the writer was worth cultivating. Goodman was at this time looking for someone to take Dan De Quille's place as local editor in the fall. "Josh" seemed a likely replacement. In late July, Goodman asked William Barstow, his business manager, to write Clemens and offer him a job as local reporter.

Clemens was not unprepared for the *Enterprise* reporting post. He was familiar with newspaper and printing work. At thirteen, following the death of his father, Clemens was taken out of school and made a printer's apprentice in order to help support his family. He learned to set type, to print and became familiar with newspaper work. He continued educating himself through serious reading. By fifteen he had read the entire Bible and many of the works of Cervantes, Dickens, Goldsmith and Hood. After he found a page from a book about Joan of Arc in the street, Clemens developed a serious interest in history. Clemens was highly curious, had a precocious understanding both of words and human nature and he was a good speller.

He began writing, largely to amuse himself and by seventeen managed to publish a story in an Eastern magazine. After completing his apprenticeship, Clemens worked for two of Orion's newspapers as a printer and editor and occasionally wrote humorous articles in which he made fun of local characters.

When he turned eighteen, Clemens began traveling throughout eastern America. In each city where he stayed he found newspaper work as a printer or compositor. For two newspapers, the Muscatine, Iowa *Journal* and the Keokuk, Iowa *Daily Post,* Clemens worked as correspondent and regularly sent letters of his travels for which he was paid $5 each. In 1859 and 1861 while Clemens was a river pilot, he published humorous sketches in the New Orleans *Crescent.* Horace Bixby, who taught Clemens to pilot steamboats, said that when Sam wasn't piloting he was "always scribbling." Even before Goodman's offer arrived, Clemens had toyed with the idea of writing for the Sacramento *Union* or the Carson *Age* and he had asked Orion to intervene on his behalf.

Like many incidents in the life of Sam Clemens, Goodman's job offer arrived at the right time. Clemens was discouraged with silver mining. Buying and developing mining claims had drained he and Orion's meager funds. The emotional ups and downs were nerve racking; one day believing he would be a millionaire, the next day wondering how to pay the grocer. Broke, Clemens went to work in a stamp mill smashing rock with a sledge hammer and shoveling it into a battery. The experience was humbling and got Clemens' attention:

> *...I will remark, in passing, that I only remained in the milling business one week. I told my employer I could not stay longer without an advance in my wages; that I liked quartz milling, indeed was infatuated with it; that I had never before grown so tenderly attached to an occupation in so short a time; that nothing, it seemed to me, gave such scope to intellectual activity as feeding a battery and screening tailings, and nothing so stimulated the moral attributes as retorting bullion and washing blankets still, I felt constrained to ask an increase in salary.*
>
> *He said he was paying me ten dollars a week, and thought it a good round sum. How much did I want?*
>
> *I said about four hundred thousand dollars a month, and board,*

was about all I could reasonably ask, considering the hard times.

I was ordered off the premises! And yet, when I look back to those days and call to mind the exceeding hardness of the labor I performed in that mill, I only regret that I did not ask him seven hundred thousand."

Roughing It

Sam Clemens had believed his Aurora silver mines would make he and Orion millionaires. Now Goodman's offer as a local reporter on the *Enterprise* for a paltry $25 a week seemed like Paradise.

"...I wanted to fall down and worship him now. Twenty-Five Dollars a week--it looked like bloated luxury--a fortune, a sinful and lavish waste of money. But my transports cooled when I thought of my inexperience and consequent unfitness for the position--and straightaway on top of this, my long array of failures rose up before me. Yet if I refused this place I must presently become dependent upon somebody for my bread, a thing necessarily distasteful to a man who had never experienced such humiliation since he was thirteen years old...So I was scared into being a city editor. I would have declined otherwise. Necessity is the mother of "taking chances."

Roughing It

September 9, Clemens wrote his last letter from Aurora to Billy Claggett. "Billy," he said, "I can't stand another winter in this climate, unless I am obliged to...I don't think much of the camp-- not as much as I did. Old fashioned winter & Snow lasted until the middle of June."

Unable to pay for stage fare, Sam Clemens left Aurora on foot in mid-September to begin his reporting job at Virginia City. Clemens had no idea he was walking dead broke across the Nevada desert straight into American history at Virginia City.

(For more on Clemens' experiences at Aurora, read MARK TWAIN: HIS ADVENTURES AT AURORA AND MONO LAKE, by the author.)

Carson City in the 1870's from the plaza looking west.

The Ormsby House on Carson Street in Carson City, where Sam Clemens first arrived. The Ormsby House was Carson's finest hotel. *Nevada Historical Society.*

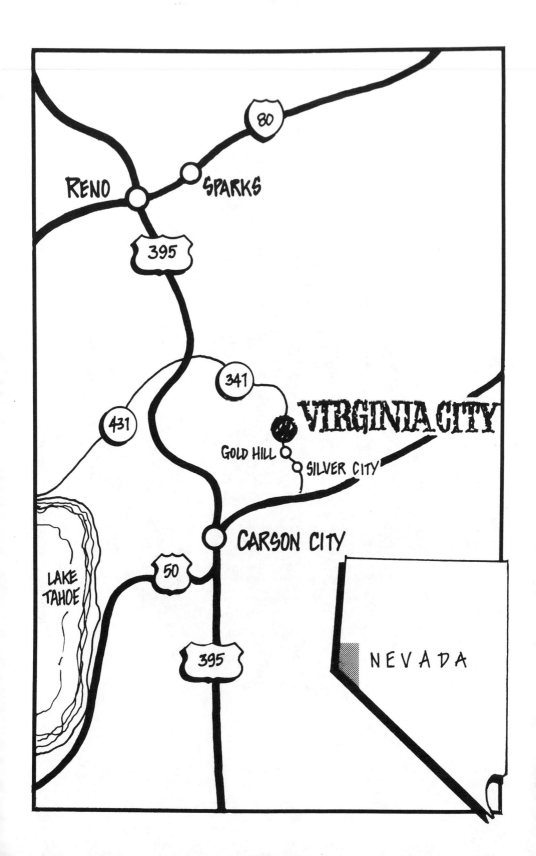

CHAPTER TWO

Virginia City, Nevada

Virginia City is located in northwestern Nevada between Carson City and Reno in the Washoe Mountains, not far from the California border. The town can be reached from the south via Carson City, from the north through Reno and from the east by Highway 50 which cuts across Nevada from Utah.

Each year thousands from across America and around the world visit Virginia City. Today the old Western mining town is world famous through the popular "Bonanza" television series. The tourist season lasts roughly from March through October though tourists visit the town even in deep winter.

From Carson City the visitor takes Highway 50 east 8 miles. Here Highway 341 leads 7 miles north into the Washoe Mountains and to Virginia City. Those with RV's or trailers find an easier grade on the truck route just past Silver City. Cars can easily make the steeper route through Gold Hill. The drive from Carson City takes about a half hour.

From Reno, you can reach Virginia City by taking highway 395 south toward Carson City. About 8 miles south of Reno a sign points southeast to Virginia City. From here two lane Highway 341 winds 12 miles up the Geiger Grade into the Washoe Mountains and to Virginia City. Though steeper and longer, the Geiger Grade route from Reno is more scenic. Photographers have a field day.

There is a vista point half way up the Geiger Grade at about 6,000 feet where you can pull off the road and take pictures. From here there is a grand view. The sky is extraordinarily blue and clear. The air is filled with the fragrance of pine nut trees that thrive at this elevation on the steep sides of the mountain. The atmosphere is clear and bright. You take a breath, view the extraordinary scenery and at once you are filled with an indescribable feeling of freedom and peace of mind. So high up in that wonderful air, cares at home seem light years away.

West, across Washoe Valley, the dark mass of the Sierra mountain range stretches for miles. Beyond the Sierra are the California gold fields and the Pacific Ocean. Most of the winter storms and precipitation come from the West across the Sierra and into Nevada. The huge forests of Sierra timber supplied Virginia City with lumber to build the town and timbers to support huge walls of rock in the hundreds of miles of mine tunnels below the town. A large section of the Sierra was entirely stripped in order to supply the mines with millions of board feet of timber. Virginia City literally sits on huge timbers that are gradually being crushed as the town slowly sinks.

Below, between the Washoe Mountains and the Sierra Nevada is Washoe Valley, green and pastoral. In the early mining days, Washoe Valley farms supplied Virginia City with vegetables and meat. Today the farms and ranches are largely recreational. Mark Twain's friend, Theodore Winters, owned a ranch in Washoe Valley. The Winters' house, currently being restored, is on the east side of highway 395 between Steamboat Hot Springs and Carson City.

Washoe Lake takes up a large portion of Washoe Valley. Its eastern shore lays at the base of the Washoe Mountains. Camping, boating, wind surfing and fishing are available at the Lake. West of Washoe Lake, Highway 395 cuts through the valley, the main artery between Reno and Carson City, 30 miles apart.

Steamboat Hot Springs is at the foot of the mountains east of 395 just south of the Geiger Grade cut-off. Steamboat Hot Springs has been a health resort since the early mining days. There Mark Twain recuperated from a severe bronchial cold and wrote several articles including, "Curing A Cold." From the highway you can see the white wisps of steam and smell the rotten odor of sulphur.

To the south, Reno is sprawled out in the Truckee Meadows surrounded by brown and barren hills. Several of the tall casino buildings can be clearly seen. At night the bright neon lights

Virginia City in the mid-1870's from the east. The California Pan Mill is in the foreground, Mt. Davidson is behind the town. *Carlton Watkins photo, California State Library.*

sparkle in the clear air. Travel time from Reno to Virginia City via Geiger Grade is about 35 minutes, longer if you stop to take pictures or have a picnic lunch at the vista point.

Virginia City, at an elevation of 6200 feet, lays at the eastern foot of Mt. Davidson, the highest of the Washoe Mountains. The mountain towers 2,000 feet above the town, brown and barren except for the ever present sagebrush and a few pine nut trees. On top of the mountain the American flag flaps back and forth in the wind on a tall iron pole placed there by the miners more than a century ago. Scattered across the mountain are piles of rust colored mine tailings. Several steep and narrow roads crisscross the mountain leading from one mine site to another. Though Mt. Davidson is the focus and backdrop for the town, no major mines were located on the mountain.

Looking down from Mt. Davidson, Virginia City appears cuddled in a cove about a mile wide cut into the foot of the mountain. The town seems to lay against the mountain like a child curled beside its mother. One of the most striking aspects, are the huge piles of mine tailings north, east and south of town, which mark the sites of the major mines.

The town is encircled by mountains. To the east, there is a narrow opening where Six Mile Canyon cuts through to a white desert valley ten miles away. Mormon emigrants passed through this valley in the early 1850's and discovered gold in the stream beds which lead down from the Washoe Mountains and empty into the Carson River. This eventually led to the discovery of rich deposits of gold and silver near Virginia City in 1859.

Beyond the white valley, a ribbon of dark trees marks the path of the Carson River as it winds through the white valley beneath the Pine Nut Mountains. On a clear day when there is no wind to stir the dust, you can see for a hundred miles down Six Mile Canyon, across the white desert floor to the mountains in the far distance. Here, high in this, great, natural amphitheater, you look out to the desert and mountains below like God looking down upon the Earth and the doings of the human race, with a strange peacefulness, feeling safe from all the harm the world below could bring a human life.

The town is laid out on a steep plateau which slants rapidly to the east. Standing on the steep streets of Virginia City looking east, the

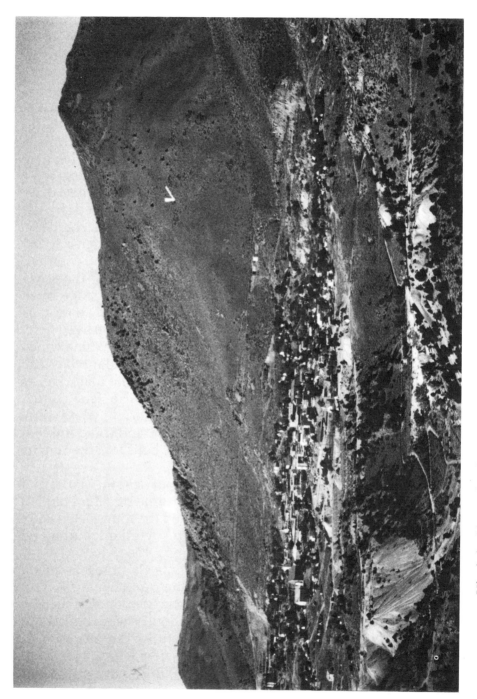

Virginia City today from the northeast. Notice the increased growth of trees. *Photo by Larry Tanner.*

entire countryside seems to slope down toward Six Mile Canyon, like a huge funnel almost as if the Canyon wanted to suck down the mountains surrounding you. Half way down Six Mile Canyon, the huge dome of Sugarloaf Mountain stands like a great brown thumb jutting out of the earth.

Streets running horizontally across the mountain are lettered; A Street is the highest. The lettered streets are terraces cut into the mountain. With the hillside so steep, one looks out his front window and down on his neighbor's roof across the street. The cross streets running up and down the mountain are so steep, some vehicles cannot make the grade even in summer. Four wheel drive vehicles are required in winter to climb the snow covered streets.

Highway 341 enters town from the north via Geiger grade and from the south from Carson City through Gold Hill. Highway 341 becomes C Street, Virginia City's main thoroughfare and commercial district. C Street is a mile long, about the width of the town. Each side of C Street is lined with two and three story brick buildings and narrow wooden buildings. Some buildings date back to the first mining boom in the 1860's when Mark Twain lived here. Most buildings were built after the Great Fire of 1875 which wiped out a large portion of the town including the Catholic church which was dynamited to prevent the fire from entering the major mines where it would have been impossible to extinguish. The church was rebuilt in brick. With its tall bell tower and bright white spire, St. Mary's In The Mountains is the tallest and predominant building in town. Every hour on the hour the bells toll; the ringing can be heard anywhere in town.

There are two other churches, the Episcopal near St. Mary's and the Presbyterian on South C Street, a wood frame structure built in the 1860's. On some summer evenings when the tourists have left and the town is still, one may pass the Presbyterian church and hear the organist practicing hymns for Sunday's services.

Between 700 and 900 people make Virginia City their home today. They live in the residential sections above and below C Street in clapboard cottages and great Victorian mansions once owned by rich mine owners or lucky investors. Most houses were built more than a century earlier. Many have been carefully restored, foundations and floors replaced, new roofs erected, new wiring and plumbing installed. There are a few old, vacant buildings, naked of paint and care. Once the town was filled with them, but new blood, mostly young and middle aged people who have fled from dangerous and noisy cities, have purchased the vacant buildings, restored and made them their homes.

The narrow cottages with steep roofs and the Victorian mansions cause the town to look like a mid-nineteenth century, eastern American village. The Victorian architecture, the small village-like town, the protection of the surrounding mountains and the friendly people give one a cozy, safe feeling.

Looking east across Virginia City. Six Mile Canyon is on the left. St. Mary's In The Mountains Church is in the middle. Piles of sand are mine dumps.

Some have lived here for decades. Some were born here and their descendants were miners or local businessmen. A large number are newcomers, mostly exiles from California who tired of the rat race and superficial values of the golden state. They discovered in Virginia City and in its people, a friendly, down to earth, quality lacking in their lives. Some left high paying jobs to move here; some left modern cities where conveniences had spoiled them and left them little to struggle for. Today many young families have moved to Virginia City because it is a safe place to raise children. Some say there are now more children than adults. There are an elementary and a high school. Since classes are smaller, each student gets lots of attention. All who moved here wanted a major change in their lives. They came to Virginia City seeking refuge. There is safety and peace of mind here; people here seem to value these more than money or material wealth.

The people who live her exemplify the Western spirit. They are highly independent, free living, fun loving, tolerant, open. There are artists of all sorts, writers, painters, sculptors, musicians, and others. One young man left an executive position in a drug store chain, moved up here and became a sign painter and book illustrator. Some local musicians perform in the saloons. Some writers self-publish local history books and sell them in the gift shops. Some worked for others for many years and found no satisfaction in it. They moved here and opened their own small businesses. They work harder than they have ever worked, struggle more than they have in years, but they are happy; people seem to feel best when they commit themselves and struggle to attain a worthwhile goal.

Altogether it is not an easy place to make a living. Except for County jobs, the local economy is entirely tourist based, the tourist season at best lasts about eight months. There are fewer jobs and they do not pay as well as in California. Most have sacrificed materially in order to live here.

Many work for local businesses. Some work for Storey County in the various county jobs, Virginia City being the County seat. Some are forced to work down the "hill" in Carson City or Reno.

During winter when there are fewer tourists, some businesses close for one or two months and their owners take vacations to warmer climates. Those employed by these businesses may leave town for winter to return in spring. Others may have saved enough to carry them through the winter.

During the tourist season, the town begins to fill around 9 AM and crowding peaks about 2 PM. All the parking spaces and lots along C Street are filled. The overflow finds parking in the large dirt lots on E Street. Soon the dirt lots are filled with RV's, trucks, trailers and cars. People hike up the steep cross streets to the central business district on C Street.

During the tourist season, C Street is like a carnival. Throngs of visitors mill down the wooden boardwalks as if walking into the mid-nineteenth century when Virginia City was considered the richest place on earth. Though the miners and outlaws who once populated the town are gone, there's plenty to remind one of Virginia City's days as a wild and reckless Western mining town.

In the old days there was a saloon every other door on C Street for a mile. Today there are still plenty of saloons. Here beside long, fine wood bars, visitors sip cocktails and beers between playing the slots or blackjack. Behind the bar is usually a large ornately carved wooden back bar with a huge mirror. Unlike many of today's bars, the bottles of liquor sit on shelves below the mirror. They are not shelved across the back bar up to the ceiling as if they are the main attraction. The big ornate bar and the huge saloon with its high ceiling transport the visitor to the time when miners filled the saloon. At one end of the bar, huge quarter pound hot dogs, one of the more popular snacks, slowly rotate between silver rods in the automatic cooker.

Outside the saloons, visitors clomp down the wooden boardwalks going in and out of the many shops along C Street. There are T-shirt shops, photography studios where people can dress in old West garb and have their pictures taken, blown glass shops, old West book shops, restaurants, leather gift shops, brass gifts shops, art galleries, shooting galleries, rock shops, museums, turquoise shops, casinos and of course, plenty of saloons. Banjo and honky tonk piano stream out of the Red Garter Saloon; Dixieland jazz blares from the two story, Bucket of Blood Saloon. The music mixes with the laughter and talk of excited visitors, the winning sound of slot machine bells and coins clinking into metal catchers. The sweet, intoxicating smells of freshly made candy and fruit cobblers flows from some doorways. Everyone seems happy, thrilled to be in a place where one is treated like an adult. If you want to gamble all of your money away, you can. If you want to get roaring drunk, you can. Out-of-staters revel in the seeming looseness and high wire adventure.

Around 5 PM the visitors begin leaving town and by 8, Virginia City resumes its quiet, peaceful life. After work, locals gather in the many restaurants and saloons. It is as if the locals re-inhabit the town. In these after hours one can really get to know Virginia City and the people who live there.

The Union Brewery Saloon is a favorite haunt for locals. It's the sort of saloon Mark Twain and his drinking cronies would have frequented. Whenever in town, I stop by the Union Brewery; not so much for the booze but for the people, the laughter, the music, the conversation and the good times. The Union Brewery embodies that wonderful quality I call the Nevada spirit. This is something few visitors get to know because most do not spend more than five or six hours in Virginia City, and that time is largely spent shopping or gambling.

The Union Brewery is on the east side of C Street at the far north end of town. It's on the C Street level of a three story brick building that probably dates back to the 1870's. The entrance is two tall bare wood doors with frosted windows that look like they've been around since God created the Earth. Gordon Lane, who ran the Union Brewery for about twenty-five years and to whom much of the Brewery's legend is due, used to leave the doors open in the summer but placed a wooden stool in the doorway as if to tell tourists the place was closed. Of course it wasn't, but the stool had a way of keeping the less daring, feeble visitor out and I suppose that's what Gordon wanted. It seems, only persons of character made their way into the Union Brewery. Usually Gordon's German shepard was sprawled asleep in front of the doorway. Most visitors would stop at the doorway and cautiously peek inside the saloon. Only the most daring thrill seeker stepped over Gordon's dog and slipped past the wooden sentry.

Once inside, the visitor found himself in what at first appeared a decrepit, sleazy dive about 20 feet wide and 30 feet deep. On the left side of the room next to the door is the bar, the legendary bar, of brown oak I think, scraped up, gnarled, stained with the beer, whisky, vodka, gin, sweat and dirt of countless persons who never had such a good time in a saloon before. Behind the bar is the traditional huge mirror which you can sort of see yourself in through the dust and grime. At the far end of the bar is an ancient freezer that hasn't worked in years. Opposite the bar is an upright piano that looks like it has seen better days but is one of the best sounding pianos I have ever played. That old piano has given myself and others countless hours of enjoyment.

The walls of the saloon were yellow or beige a couple of centuries ago. Now the paint is faded and filthy and the color is something indescribable. The walls are covered with various odd items from the past: a map of the Virginia City mines, advertisements for strange beers and liqueurs that haven't been made in years, a portrait of a beautiful young woman in a long gown which visitors marvel at and some have been known to fall in love with. Above the bar is a sign that reads: THIS IS MY DAM HOUSE AND I'LL DO AS I PLEASE. Toward the rear of the saloon is a round table on top of which is something that looks like a decayed dog. This is the monster that was used in a homemade science fiction movie and I've been told it was one of the worst films ever made.

The ceiling is about 12 feet high from which a couple of battered light fixtures dangle and sort of light the saloon at night.

Behind the bar is an old cash register whose drawer is always left half open. Instead of depositing bills in the register, the bills are thrown across the cash register, some land in the half opened drawer, most land on the keys where they pile up through the evening. Some bills slip between bottles next to the register. Some fall on the floor and are walked on all night; some bills, I've been told have been walked over for years. Money doesn't mean much here.

Gordon Lane never used a jigger or one of those mechanical guns to pour his drinks. He propped the bottle up and poured freely. Drinks were always double what you would get anywhere else and half the price. That was good business and one of the reasons so many people came back to the Union Brewery for a quarter century. A healthy scotch and soda sold for a dollar, 1.75 or $2 anywhere else.

I discovered the Union Brewery Saloon several years ago while working on another book about Virginia City. Myself and Kevin Lamb, a good friend and fellow high road adventurer, stumbled into the place sometime in the early evening after driving all day. Gordon's stool stood in the doorway of course. Naturally reckless, we slid past the sentry and entered the world of the Union Brewery. Immediatley we felt as if we had just come home.

Gordon Lane stood behind the bar with his arms outstretched leaning on the bar. He was in his early sixties but he looked a couple of decades younger, "well preserved", as one local put it. Gordon was about five foot three, tanned face, youthful eyes, sandy-grey hair combed back. He was wearing a short sleeved sports shirt and a beige colored pants, the type worn by the military. Gordon nodded and smiled as we walked in. He knew we were visitors.

We sat down on wooden stools and ordered scotch and sodas. We watched Gordon freely pour the scotch into our glasses and nodded to one another. Gordon slid our drinks to us, both a rich golden from the heavy scotch, and collected a measly dollar from each of us. We knew we were in Nevada.

I gravitated toward the old piano and cautiously played a number and when I was not asked to stop, figured it was alright. I played a selection of my Greatest Hits, a few Scott Joplin rags and a blues version of the "House of the Rising Sun." After about forty minutes, Kevin, who had by this time swallowed enough Scotch to keep Scotland solvent, came over and began howling to the piano playing. The Scotch had done its work. I liked the place and didn't want to be asked to leave so I stopped playing and Kevin quieted down to a gentle roar.

Impressed by the way we had made ourselves to home, the locals took us in. They asked us where we were from and we joked and laughed and gabbed for the rest of the evening. That was the first of many enjoyable evenings in the Union Brewery Saloon.

For all its apparent looseness, under Gordon Lane the Union Brewery had its own peculiar code of conduct. This was subltly and at times not so subtly laid down by Gordon.

Congenial drunks were tolerated and allowed to stay until they passed out. Then they were asked to leave. Trouble making drunks were asked to leave. Tourists who asked Gordon dumb questions were tolerated unless the visitor's question was particularly stupid. Gordon then threw back a smart quip or moved to the end of the bar and left the idiot visitor who continued sipping his drink unaware he had been insulted.

Women were not allowed to swear; women who did were thrown out.

Anyone could play the piano providing they could play well enough and Gordon felt like listening to it. If Gordon didn't or if you played badly, you were asked to stop.

The Union Brewery was sort of an extension of Gordon Lane. It was by nature friendly, generous, highly independent and full of goodwill. On several occasions before finishing a drink, I discovered, someone, usually a stranger, had bought me another. I recall times Gordon filled my half empty glass with Scotch and remarked, "George, let me freshen that up," and expected nothing in return. Gordon was generous and thoughtful. In a world that is all too often selfish and thoughtless, Gordon became unique and well regarded. He had a matter of fact way of making you welcome as if you were a guest in his home. Gordon made many feel this way for over a quarter century. You felt accepted, comfortable, like Gordon's place was your place so you looked forward to returning.

I guess the reason I've rattled on about the Union Brewery, is because the saloon embodies the real Virginia City, that unpretentious, honest, earthy, open spirit the adventurous young men brought to the town more than a century ago when the West was young and wild like them. More than all the books, letters, newspapers and articles I studied attempting to discover Mark Twain's life in Virginia City, the closest I came to experiencing his life there, were the evenings I spent in the Union Brewery with a Scotch, some piano playing and the fine conversation and laughter supplied by the locals. For it was in Virginia City saloons like the Union Brewery where Twain drank and lived, collected news, laughed, shared his strange stories and there began to sense his own talent and powers.

The Union Brewery today is as much like the early saloons as one could hope to find. The saloon becomes a common ground for people who would otherwise have nothing in common. Here a person is not esteemed by how much money he earns, by the clothes on his back nor by his profession but by his character; character is what is important. Here the truck driver has little trouble conversing with the lawyer. Stepping into the Union Brewery, one is forced to leave his public facade outside. It does not fit here and it will not impress anyone. But the people here are so friendly and genuine you feel no need to hide behind that face you grudgingly wear back in the push-and-shove city. That life suddenly seems light years away, meaningless and superficial. These people, their openess, these jokes, this laughter, this drink, that piano playing, that cigar smoke, that fragrance from the wood burning stove; this is real, genuine. You feel safe. This is refuge. The most cynical city dweller must leave the Union Brewery Saloon feeling like he has visited one of the finest spots in the world. And he has.

Some of the most interesting people in the world step through the doors of the Union Brewery Saloon some time after 3:00 PM each day. On one of my last visits I met a couple from New Orleans where they own a unique gift shop. They travel all over the world three months each year collecting primitive art and rare religious artifacts which they sell in their store. The man had been visiting the Union Brewery Saloon for twenty years on vacations. The three of us talked for several hours and became friends. I'm certain I'll run into them again in the Brewery and it will be like time has not passed. Nearly every time I visit the Brewery I meet someone I wouldn't have otherwise met and end up talking for hours. The goodwill is contagious; you feel comfortable and open.

Recently, Gordon Lane stepped down from the saloon business but I understand the new owner intends to continue the friendly traditions of the Union Brewery Saloon.

C Street, Virginia City around 1910. The Territorial Enterprise building is noted in the photo as "Mark Twain's Office". *Nevada Historical Society.*

CHAPTER THREE

Mark Twain's Virginia City

The Virginia City, Sam Clemens walked into in 1862, was a child about three years old, a hodge podge of canvas tents, dugouts in the hillsides, stone cabins, frame cabins and one and two story wood frame buildings. The dirt streets were swamps when it rained and dust bowls during dry weather, clogged day and night by huge freight wagons and teams of horses and mules and men on horeseback. One risked his life attempting to cross the street. Until recently, supplies had been packed in on animals up the steep mountain paths. Finally a decent road was carved out of the mountain and wagons were able to make the grade. With the new wagons badly needed supplies arrived, lumber, feed, mining supplies, vegetables and meat. The town flourished. It was filled with frenzied miners, speculators, businessmen and armed killers looking for their next victims. Three years ago there was nothing here but sagebrush, rock and a few pine nut trees. Now a great mining town was taking shape on a steep mountainside in the middle of nowhere. The discovery of rich deposits of gold and silver brought these men here. This is how it happened:

In the spring of 1850, a Mormon emigrant party camped beside the Carson River near what is now Dayton. They were on the emigrant road from Utah west across Nevada to California. The road happened to pass through the sandy flats between the Washoe and Pine Nut mountains along the Carson River. They intended to reach Placerville but had learned the mountain passes were still snowed in. They decided to camp beside the river under the cottonwoods until the passes cleared.

The Mormons were camped near the mouth of Gold Canyon. With little to do, some men ventured up the Canyon and began panning for gold. They discovered enough gold dust to pay for beans and bacon but not enough to make them stay. With visions of greater fortunes awaiting them in the California gold fields, the Mormon party moved on and left their discovery.

Not long afterward, Spofford Hall built a log house at what is now Dayton near the mouth of Gold Canyon. This was the first permanent settlement in the region. The place came to be know as Hall's Station, later McMartin's Station. Here weary emigrants bought or traded for needed supplies.

Word of the Gold Canyon placer discovery was passed on to others. By the spring of 1852, a considerable number were working the lower portion of the Canyon where they made $5 to $10 a day in their rockers. The following spring, their number increased to 200-300. During winter and spring there was enough water in the Canyon to placer mine. But in summer there was little or no water and only fifty or so stayed to work the Canyon.

As the lower portion was worked out, miners pushed farther into the Canyon. The hamlet of Johntown was built a few miles up the Canyon, a sorry collection of stone and log buildings. From 1856-58 Johntown was the center of mining activity. Here the miners gathered after work at "Dutch Nick's", Nick Ambrose's store, where a horrible form of whisky was sold called "tarantula juice"--strong enough to kill rattle snakes or spiders if a man was bitten. Ambrose supplied the miners with room and board, that is, food and a blanket for about $10-14 a week. A miner found the nearest clump of sagebrush and curled up with his blanket underneath the stars. "Dutch Nick" would later find his way into one of Mark Twain's famous hoaxes, the "Massacre At Dutch Nick's."

In 1852, Edgar Allen and Hosea B. Grosch, brothers, built a stone cabin about one mile above Johntown near Silver City. The Grosch brothers had considerable knowledge of mining and metalurgy. They brought with them a collection of scientific books, furnaces for smelting and testing and chemicals and equipment for assaying. The brothers kept to themselves and spoke little of their mining claims. It was later learned the Groschs believed there were rich silver deposits in the area and were believed to have made the first discovery of silver ore near Mt. Davidson.

But in 1857, Hosea while mining, severely injured his foot with a pick. Within several days, he died of infection. Allen, in his grief, left the area and attempted to cross the Sierra in the winter. Both his feet were frozen and amputated. He died shortly after from the shock of the operation. With the Grosch brothers died the whereabouts of the rich silver ore deposits.

In January, 1859, there was a spell of good weather. The Johntowners spread out and began prospecting. Saturday, January 28, 1859, Henry "Old Pancake" Comstock, John Bishop, James "Old Virginia" Finney and others struck surface diggings at the head of Gold Canyon at the sight of today's Gold Hill, about one mile south of Virginia City. The men claimed the diggings for placer mining and did not know beneath them was one of the richest bodies of silver and gold ore in the world. Working the Gold Hill surface diggings, the miners now made $15-20 a day. The rest of the Johntowners eventually moved up to Gold Hill. Nick Ambrose followed his clientele. Gold Hill later became the sight of some of the richest Comstock mines: Belcher, Crown Point, Yellow Jacket, Imperial and Kentuck.

Six Mile Canyon, one mile north of Gold Canyon, runs parallel to Gold Canyon and leads down from Mt. Davidson to the flats near the Carson River. Gold had also been discovered in Six Mile Canyon and miners had gradually worked their way up the Canyon to the foot of Mt. Davidson. Two of these miners were Irishmen, Peter O'Riley and Pat McLaughlin.

June 1, 1859, O'Riley and McLaughlin were working at the head of Six Mile Canyon at what is today called the Ophir Pit, at the north end of Virginia City above A Street. O'Riley and McLaughlin were making a paltry $1.50-2.00 a day and were about to try elsewhere. But they decided to work their claim a few more days. To conserve water, they dug a hole for a reservoir. They had dug down about four feet when they struck a mass of black, decomposed silver ore. They did not know what the strange black stuff was but figured it was worth washing. They were astonished when the first pan of black dirt produced a thick coating of gold dust. O'Riley and McLaughlin excitedly continued washing pan after pan of the

Offices of Shaw's Fast Freight Line in the 1860's from which Mark Twain left and returned to Virginia City. *Nevada Historical Society.*

black sand until evening.

While they were cleaning up, Henry "Old Pancake" Comstock showed up. He had been searching the area for a stray pony which he found and was atop of when he stumbled across the Irishmen. Comstock, who had a keen eye for other men's goods, immediately saw the pile of gold dust O'Riley and McLaughlin had produced during the day's washings. Comstock hopped from his pony and ran his hands through the pile of gold dust. Greedy and manipulative, he now set about to steal what he desired. Comstock told O'Riley and McLaughlin they were on his "ranch." Though he had nothing to prove it, he claimed he owned the property they were mining. Not only were they working his land but they were using his water. Comstock demanded that they cut him and his friend, Manny (Emmanuel) Penrod in on the claim. The Irishmen did not want trouble and they were unaware how rich their claim was. They agreed to give interests in their claim to Comstock and his friend. The discovery was called the Ophir. The original locators were filed as Peter O'Riley, Patrick McLaughlin, H.T.P. Comstock, E. Penrod and J.A. (Kentuck) Osborne. The men named each had one sixth of 1,400 feet of ground on the lead; Comstock and Penrod were given an additional 100 feet to split. The entire Ophir claim amounted to 1,500 feet. Comstock and Penrod's additional 100 feet became known as the Mexican or Spanish mine. The ravine has since been known as Spanish Ravine.

Where previously O'Riley and McLaughlin were making a $1.50-2.00 a day, now they were hauling out $1,000 in gold each day, literally pounds of it. They still did not know what the heavy black sand was and continually cursed it and threw it aside because it interfered with the washing of the gold.

In July, Augustus Harrison, a rancher from the Truckee Meadows, took a sample of the black sand to Grass Valley where it was assayed. The black sand turned out to be a rich form of silver sulfide and would yield several thousands of dollars per ton in gold and silver.

Harrison tried to keep the discovery quiet but he told a friend who told a friend and immediately there was a mass exit of California miners for the Washoe mountains.

At first the new discovery site was called Pleasant Hill, then Mt. Pleasant Point, Ophir and Ophir Diggins. But in November, 1859,

The International Hotel at the northwest corner of Union and C streets about the time Mark Twain lived here. The International was the finest hotel west of the Mississippi. Mark Twain and Dan De Quille shared an apartment on B Street a few doors down from the International. *Nevada Historical Society.*

James "Old Virginia" Finney, while on a drinking spree with other miners, fell and broke his whisky bottle. "I baptise this ground Virginia," he said and since then the town has been known as Virginia City.

In time the Ophir was discovered to be part of a lode of silver ore that stretched 3 miles and was 100 feet wide at its broadest point. The Comstock Lode, named after crazy Henry Comstock, stretched north and south beneath the eastern base of Mt. Davidson. Virginia City was at the north end of the Comstock Lode literally built on top of the richest portion. Gold Hill was at the southern end a mile away across the Divide. In time, Virginia City, Gold Hill, Silver City and American Flat merged into one mining community known as the Comstock.

Since 1861, the Comstock mines have produced more than 400 million dollars. The tremendous wealth helped the Union win the Civil War and financed the building of San Francisco. Sam Clemens arrived in mid-September just in time for the first boom in 1863. Between 1863-67 the Comstock mines yielded 20 million dollars. During the spectacular "Bonanza" years, 1873-80, the Comstock mines produced more than 300 million dollars in gold and silver.

Virginia City eventually reached a population of 25,000, crammed into a town about a mile square. Where other mining towns were wooden and men eked out a bare existence, Virginia City was largely brick and miners were paid well and lived well. Miners earned $4-$6 day and this was considered good pay. The town was cosmopolitan, rich and proud. Stores were stocked with the best merchandise. Restaurants were the finest west of New York. Here miners feasted on well prepared quality food from oysters to prime rib; most restaurants had well stocked wine cellars.

C Street became the main thoroughfare and central business district. On both sides were wooden and brick buildings, some five stories high. Here were located shops and businesses of every sort: grocery stores, meat markets, livery stables, saloons, brokerage houses, tailors, banks, jewelery stores, boarding houses, hotels and others. A person could find just about anything he wanted. Mine superintendents, merchants and professional men lived on A and B Streets in ornate mansions. Miners lived with their families in hundreds of tiny shacks clustered around the mines below D

Street.

In their off hours, miners filled the saloons. When Mark Twain lived here there were 51 saloons, over 100 during the 1870's. Miners consumed liquor in huge quantities, mostly wine, beer and whisky. Miners found amusement in the three redlight districts, dance halls, hurdy houses and in Piper's and Maguires opera houses where traveling actors and musicians entertained.

For twenty years Virginia City's silver mines were known throughout America. For fifteen years they affected the lives of Americans everywhere, sometimes remotely sometimes directly with the rise and fall of their fortunes. Virginia City became a Promised Land to thousands who flocked there believing their fortunes could be made over night. Some lives, like Mark Twain's, became wonderful success stories. But many did not fare so well; there are many tales of terrible tragedies.

Virginia City was extraordinarily rich in men of character. They were for the most part, adventurous, intelligent, gifted and most were in their twenties. They were drawn to Virginia City by the opportunity the town offered. Virginia City was a place where the American Dream could become reality with initiative, hard work and a bit of luck. Wells Drury, an *Enterprise* writer, recalls the early days:

> *There was a deal of drinking in Virginia when the* Enterprise *and the town were new, but it wasn't all drinking. Some of the brightest men of the country were working as well as having fun there. Lawyers...admit the bar was about the brainiest ever gathered together in one town of the size, or ten times the size. Adventurers, with keen wits and empty pockets, were drawn there as naturally as gamblers seek a faro-room. Rolling stones of every kind obeyed the moral law of gravitation by rolling up to Mt. Davidson. It was a city of men. If any of them were poor that troubled them not at all, for they expected to be rich by next week and had good ground for the expectation. Those who were rich had so recently been poor that they had forgotten it, and the circumstance was not so unusual as to be deemed a title to others' deference. Everyone was rated for what he was not what he had. There were no classes, only individuals. Pretension was out of order. Not to be a man of sense, frank, free-handed and without*

prejudices, was to find oneself a second or third grader. The men most distinguished for ability were the best fellows, the heartiest roysterers, the most democratic. Money was no object. There were oceans of it underground.

Virginia City was the grandest and richest mining town in the American West during the nineteenth century. Built in the middle of the barren Nevada desert on the side of a high mountain, it radiated in the isolated wilderness like a great golden city suspended in the sky.

Maguire's Opera House is the two story building just right of the flag pole. Here Mark Twain was presented the fake meerschaum pipe by Steve Gillis and other *Enterprise* **jokesters December 1863.** *Nevada Historical Society.*

CHAPTER FOUR

The Territorial Enterprise

The *Territorial Enterprise*, began humbly as a scrawny Western journal. Within several years, the *Enterprise* became the most influential newspaper on the West Coast and the primary source of Western news for Eastern papers.

The *Territorial Enterprise* was the first newspaper published between Salt Lake City and the western slope of the Sierra Nevada. W.L. Jernegan and Alfred James published the first issue December 18, 1858 in Genoa, Nevada, then known as Mormon Station. Genoa was a farming settlement of about 200 people in the Carson Valley at the foot of the Sierra, 15 miles southwest of Carson City. Today travelers pass the quaint town on the way to Lake Tahoe or Placerville.

During the 1850's, Genoa was the last supply station for emigrants before crossing the Sierra to Placerville, California. Genoa was not large enough to financially support the *Territorial Enterprise* profitably; for six months Jernegan and James struggled to keep the paper afloat. "Snowshoe" Thompson, who carried the mail back and forth between Genoa and Placerville, supplied Jernegan and James with firsthand California news and carried on his back the very paper the *Enterprise* was printed on.

Following the discovery of gold and silver at Virginia City in June, 1859, Jernegan and James moved the *Enterprise* to Carson City. In January, 1860, Jonathan Williams bought out James. In October, Williams, who apparently had become sole owner, moved the *Enterprise* to Virginia City where he published the paper once a week.

Williams' *Enterprise* was on its last legs when twenty-three year old Joe Goodman and twenty year old Dennis McCarthy showed up from San Francisco. On March 2, 1861, with $40 dollars between them, Goodman and McCarthy bought the *Enterprise*, type, fixtures and all for $1,000 on time. They turned the weekly into an eight page daily published each morning six days a week, Monday through Saturday. The *Enteprise* kept this format for thirty-two years. The *Enterprise* sold for ten cents daily; subscription rates were $16 a year in advance, $10 for six months, $6 for three months.

The *Territorial Enterprise* was first published in Virginia City in a rickety one story frame building thirty-five feet long and twenty feet wide on the northwest corner of A Street and Sutton Avenue. B Street was at that time the central business district. Dan De Quille became a reporter for the *Enterprise* in 1862 and remained with the paper until publication suspended in 1893. DeQuille recalls life and work in the *Enterprise's* first one room office:

"...In this room was the press (one of the old-fashioned Washington presses), the cases of the compositors, the desk of the book-keeper, the tables of the editors, and all the belongings of the office. On the north side of the main building was a shed addition which was both kitchen and dining room, and besides was fitted up as a sleeping place for all hands. Along the sides of the walls 'bunks' were arranged one above another, as on shipboard, and as in the cabins of the miners of California in the early days.

A Chinaman (Old Joe), officiated as cook and acted as waiter during meals. A table some fifteen feet in length occupied the center of the shed, and on this were always to be found all of the substantials and most of the luxuries obtainable in the market, served up in Old Joe's best style.

The old Chinaman was long thought to be the 'boss' cook of the town...chiefly for the reason that he was able to place the butter on the table moulded into the forms of lions, dragons, and the like. So much was said in praise of Joe's lions, tigers, and dragons, that he finally gave most of his time to the modeling of such works of art. Presently mouse hairs began to be found in the biscuits every morn-

ing and flies and bugs in other articles of food. An investigation brought to light two or three dead mice in Joe's lard keg, where he had for a week or two been pouring back into the keg hot fat without discoverng the four-legged game that had been trapped from time to time. Other equally unpleasant discoveries were made, and Joe was 'fired out' by acclamation. Other Chinamen followed but as all hands were now constantly on the watch for faults in the cookery, none remained long, and presently cooking in the office was discontinued, and the employees dispersed to try their luck among the restaurants.

While the kitchen was running it was a standing joke to invite some aquaintance about the town to dinner in order to try experiments by which to test the strength of his stomach. No sooner had the stranger commenced eating than some one began to tell about some disgusting thing calculated to impair his appetite. More than one guest was driven from the table amid the laughter of the case-hardened regular boarders...All this time they little suspected the kind of messes that were being dealt out to them at home by Old Joe, whose ways had not been discovered yet.

The office did very well in summer, but in winter it was as full of discomforts as any place seen by Dante during his journey through the infernal regions. There were not only extremes of heat and cold, but one often suffered from both at the same moment--would be freezing on one side and burning on the other. On very cold nights the stove would be made red hot. Around it the editors drew up their tables, and the printers moved their cases as near as they could get them. They stood at their cases with old barley sacks lashed around their feet with pieces of bailing rope, and were frequently obliged to go to the stove and thaw out their half frozen fingers.

At times, too, when the snow began to thaw off the roof, there were leaks all over the office. Strings were then fastened up against the roof at the worst leaks, and the water led down to the floor at the sides of the building, thus carrying it over and beyond the tables and cases. At times so many of these strings were in use that the ceiling and all the upper part of the office had the appearance of being hung with huge cobwebs...

...There was then no telegraph line across the continent, and all Eastern and European news came by 'Pony Express.' Before the 'Pony' was put on, all news came by steamer via Panama, or by the

overland stage coaches. The 'Pony,' therefore, was looked upon as being nearly lightning, and he really was the next thing to it.

The 'Pony' rider was often able to give items of news from the plains that were not in his budget, and he was always interviewed in regard to the emigrant trains that were making their way in, the movements of the Indians, and the like.

Besides looking after the news of the town, the local editors also interviewed the 'captains' of all the pack'trains that came in over the Sierra Nevada Mountains, the teamsters, and the stage drivers, and their passengers. Also, at this time, all the country to the eastward remained to be prospected; and men who scouted out into the wilderness a distance of 100 to 300 miles always had some wonderful stories to relate in their return...

In these early days there were in town many desperate characters, and bloody affrays were of frequent occurrence. Sometimes while a reporter was engaged in gleaning the particulars in regard to one shooting scrape another would start (growing out of something said in regard to the first) and the news-gatherer suddenly found himself in the midst of flying bullets, and had before him a battle, the particulars in regard to which he need not take at second-hand...

Thompson and West's, History of Nevada

Early in 1862, the *Enterprise* moved to 27 north C where the Silver Queen Casino stands today. The *Enterprise* was next door to the Wells Fargo Express office. While located here, Sam Clemens joined the paper and Dennie (Jerry) Driscoll became a partner and business manager. Goodman did most of the writing occasionally assisted by Captain Joe Plunkett. McCarthy was in charge of layout and printing. Dan De Quille and Clemens were the local editors. During this time, Rollin M. Daggett wrote part time for the paper. Steve Gillis was a compositor and printer.

In July, 1863, the *Territorial Enterprise* was moved into its new three story brick building on the east side of South C Street between Union and Taylor. The *Enterprise* building stands today though it has been through several fires. Here Mark Twain wrote from August, 1863 until late May, 1864. Today there is a Mark Twain museum in the basement where the old steam powered presses can be seen.

The Silver Queen Casino marks the site of the second *Territorial Enterprise* **offices where Mark Twain first went to work for the paper.** *Larry Tanner Photo.*

Once in the new building, the *Enterprise* employed steam powered presses and twenty printers were hired to operate the machines. Goodman, turned much of the editorial work over to George Dawson, an Englishman, and Rollin M. Dagget. Goodman concentrated on his poetry, theatrical reviews and controversial issues. Steve Gillis and Charles Putnam were news and telegraph editors and wrote up the Eastern and European news. For a time, "Lying" Jim Townsend was a printer though he worked for other papers as a writer and editor. Townsend, along with other *Enterprise* staff, played an important role in Mark Twain's development. Twain's, "Jumping Frog of Calaveras County" was based on a story Townsend published in the 1850's. In *Roughing It*, Twain attributes Townsend with the story of a corrupt Aurora mining company which had defrauded investors by levying unnecessry assessments. In the 1880's, Jim Townsend ran the *Homer Mining Index* at Lundy, California, a gold mining town on the slopes of the Eastern Sierra, near Mono Lake. In the 1890's he ran a paper at nearby Bodie. Some scholars attribute some of Twain's early humorous writing style and his Western stories to "Lying" Jim Townsend.

On October 28, 1863, Goodman and McCarthy became sole owners of the *Enterprise*. Dennie Driscoll left the paper to start a successful Virginia City brokerage house. In 1864, Rollin Daggett joined the paper permanently. Goodman bought out McCarthy, September 15, 1865. Four months later, McCarthy, who had lost his money in the stock market, was back at the *Enterprise* in his old job, now as an employee. Goodman remained sole owner until 1874 when he soldout to William Sharon.

Sharon, Mackay and Mills became owners and under the Enterprise Publishing Company, ran the paper until January 15, 1893 when the *Enterprise* first suspended publication due to the decline of Virginia City mines. During the latter 1870's, Rollin Daggett and Charles Goodwin were editors; Dan De Quille remained local and mining editor until the paper folded.

During the boom years, the *Enterprise* made a fortune. Advertising rates were high but businesses were happy to pay. Often Goodman turned away advertisers as there wasn't enough room in the paper. Sometimes a supplemental advertising sheet was added to meet demands. The *Enterprise* earned additional money printing

The *Territorial Enterprise* **Building, built in 1863, where Mark Twain wrote from August 1863 until May 1864.**

theater bills, wedding invitations, circulars and the like for local businesses; one of the largest accounts was Maguire's Opera House. Goodman was reported to have made as much as a $1,000 a day; for many years the paper netted $5,000 a month, this when $20 a week was considered good pay. Goodman literally carried money to the bank in buckets.

Under Joe Goodman's wise, agressive and courageous hands, the *Daily Territorial Enterprise* became a strong daily--lively, rugged, unpretentious, humorous and a defender of the underdog. The *Enterprise* was a mirror and reflected the free attitudes of the tough young mining town. The paper not only provided local, regional and national news but served as a community watch dog. If a corrupt Judge needed driving from the bench, Goodman went after his victim with extraordinary relish. Goodman tore his victim to shreds. If Goodman wasn't up to the job, he employed Rollin Daggett, the Merciless, who wasn't content to shred a victim; Daggett preferred annihilating the subject of scorn. Articles and items appeared in the *Enterprise* which today would be considered libel or slander and would culminate in suits. But the *Enterprise* was not irresponsible; those men attacked in its columns were deserving.

Joe Goodman, editor of the *Territorial Enterprise. Nevada Historical Society.*

Composing room of the *Enterprise* where Mark Twain, Dan De Quille, Joe Goodman, Steve Gillis and others gathered after the paper was put to bed to drink beer and sing songs.

The steam powered press used to publish the *Enterprise. Nevada Historical Society.*

The first mining boom in 1863 made Virginia City a focus of Western and Eastern attention. The *Enterprise*, being Virgina City's chief paper, became an important source of information for San Francisco stock brokers and thousands of investors throughout the West who owned shares in Virginia City mines. Other Western newspapers subscribed to the *Enterprise* and frequently copied news items. This practice would help establish Mark Twain's reputation on the West Coast.

The *Enterprise* became the chief source of Westen news for Eastern papers. The *New York Tribune* was one of several Eastern papers which faithfully subscribed.

Between 1861-1875, the *Territoral Enterprise*, was the most influential newspaper in the West. In size, it was often larger than San Francisco newspapers though that city's population was far greater.

Well, you can guess what this is. *Enterprise* staffers called it the "time killer."

CHAPTER FIVE

The Men of the *Enterprise*

The young men of the *Territorial Enterprise* had a lasting and remarkable effect on Sam Clemens. He would never be the same person nor see the world in the same way after knowing these men. All were in their twenties, all were bachelors at this time, all typified the raw, fun loving Western spirit important to Mark Twain's early career. All lived passionately and fully. All had terrific senses of humor; all were fun to be with. Though they were masculine, hardy and adventurous, they showed each other affection. They were friends to one another and took their loyalties and commitments to heart. They were honest, good, idealistic and highly creative.

Their work on the *Enterprise* gave them a sense of purpose and a bond that lasted their entire lives. They knew they worked for the best paper on the West Coast and it made them proud. Though they played hard and fooled around like the young men they were, they took their *Enterprise* work seriously. They were responsible journalists and tradesmen though they enjoyed pulling pranks on their readers. They were the top media men in a crowded and isolated mining town; their stands against corruption in high places and control of the Comstock by outside financial powers made them heros.

These men were true friends to Sam Clemens. They liked him and supported his work. Their influences on his budding writing career was overwhelming and remained with him the rest of his life. When old, Twain recalled with great affection his youthful, free living days on the *Enterprise* in Virginia City.

JOE GOODMAN

Tall, good looking, free spirited and charming, Joe Goodman was the heart and driving energy of the *Territorial Enterprise*. Between 1861-74, Joe Goodman was the most influential Western editor and publisher though historians have largely ignored his contributions. Thompson and West barely mention Goodman in their comprehensive, *History of Nevada*.

Much would have been different without Joe Goodman. Jonathan Williams' *Enterprise* would have likely died quietly. Virginia City and the West would have been without the paper's honest, humorous and compassionate voice. Sam Clemens would have remained a struggling silver miner. Mark Twain would not have been born nor allowed to develop his writing talent. American literature would be without *Tom Sawyer, Huckleberry Finn, Roughing It, The Innocents Abroad* and other great works. Dan De Quille would not have written, *The Big Bonanza*, a firsthand history of Virginia City on which modern historians rely. Nevada would have been without a reliable source of mining information and an independent political voice. Worse, Virginia City miners would have not had the daily dose of humor and good sense the *Enterprise* provided.

Joe Goodman was born in Masonville, New York, September 18, 1838. He came to California in 1856 with his father. Like other *Enterprise* writers, Goodman began working young, was largely self-educated and well read. In San Francisco at the age of eighteen Goodman found work as a typesetter at the *Golden Era*, the first literary journal on the Pacific Coast established by Rollin M. Daggett in 1852. Nearly every West Coast writer who became successful wrote for the *Era*; Mark Twain, Bret Harte and Dan De Quille were three of many. Goodman learned the printing and publishing business working for the *Golden Era* and there he cut his literary teeth writing articles and poetry under the influence of writers of character and high ideals. Goodman met and became friends with Rollin M. Daggett and Dennis E. "Mac" McCarthy who were important to the success of the *Enterprise* in its heyday. While working for the *Golden Era*, Goodman continued educating himself by avid reading, poetry, his favorite.

Sometime while working for the *Golden Era* or afterward, Good-

Joe Goodman.

man tried his hand at gold mining. Nearly every young man living on the West Coast at that time could be seduced by the intoxicating fantasy of sudden wealth. Goodman, like many, had no great success at gold mining but he apparently enjoyed the commaderie, fun and excitement of mining camp life.

In 1861, Virgina City was the most well known and exciting mining camp in Nevada Territory. Hoping to make his fortune, Goodman struck out for the silver camp with Dennis McCarthy. Goodman was twenty-three. He had never run a newspaper, never operated a business and he had little money. But Goodman was a versatile writer, able to knock out a stream of poetry as easily as prose; he was intelligent and had a clear vision of what a newspaper should be. And, he was willing to take a risk.

Goodman and McCarthy arrived at the right place at the right time. Jonathan Williams was ready to take on Goodman and McCarthy as partners. Virginia City was rapidly growing and needed a strong newspaper to provide local mining and regional news. The *Territorial Enterprise* needed the energy and vision of two young men like Goodman and McCarthy. Goodman took on the editorial responsibilities; McCarthy ran the pressroom. In six months Goodman and McCarthy turned the dying paper around and bought out Jonathan Williams.

Under Goodman's command, the *Enterprise* became highly popular. In time with a large number of paying subscribers and high advertising rates, the paper was financially successful. But Goodman and McCarthy were not wise money managers. Jerry Driscoll became a partner and businss manager; after Driscoll sold out, William Barstow took his place. Dan De Quille remarked the paper seemed to run itself; it was necessary only to dump news into the paper each day, six days a week.

Goodman deplored the control of Comstock financing by San Francisco stock brokers and bankers and retaliated in his columns. His independent stance made him a Comstock hero. William Sharon was often the object of Goodman's fiery words. Sharon was hired by William Ralston to manage the Virginia City branch of the Bank of California. At first Sharon seemed a godsend as he loaned struggling mining companies thousands of dollars at low interest rates. Mining companies spent their loans on new mining equipment, wages and mining exploration. When the money was gone they turned to Sharon for help.

But now Sharon was a different man, cold, calculating, merciless. He would loan no more money. As mining company after mining company defaulted on their loans, Sharon acquired control of Comstock mines and mills. Sharon then invested large sums in the mines and some became very successful. But it made William Sharon the most despised man in Virginia City.

When William Sharon returned to Virginia City in a bid for U. S. Senator, Joe Goodman welcomed him back. Listen:

Your unexpected return, Mr. Sharon, has afforded no opportunity for public preparation, and you will consequently accept these simple remarks as an unworthy but earnest expression of the sentiments of a people who feel they would be lacking in duty and self-respect if they failed upon such an occasion to make a deserved recognition of your acts and character. You are probably aware that you have returned to a community where you are feared, hated and despised.

Your characther in Nevada for the past nine years has been one of merciless rapacity. You fastened yourself upon the vitals of the State like a hyena, and woe to him who disputed with you a single morsel of your prey... You cast honor, honesty, and the commonest civilities aside, You broke faith with men whenever you could subserve your purpose by so doing...

Goodman's stand against Sharon in the columns of the *Enterprise* prevented Sharon from winning his bid for Senator in 1872. Sharon was forced to buy the paper in 1874 in order to stifle Goodman's attacks. Afterward, the *Enterprise* became a Sharon supporter. Sharon finally won his coveted Senate seat.

After Goodman sold the *Enterprise* in 1874, he moved to San Francisco and invested heavily in stocks. Like McCarthy, years before, he went broke. With a loan from John Mackay, he went into the vineyard business but that enterprise failed as well.

In 1884, Goodman started the *San Franciscan*, a literary weekly. The *San Franciscan* floundered; Goodman sold out and spent his remaining years studying Myan archaeology spending considerable time in Central America.

Though Joe Goodman discovered Mark Twain and allowed him

to develop his writing craft while earning a salary on the *Enterprise*, Joe Goodman never boasted of this. He and Mark Twain corresponded and remained friends until Twain's death in April, 1910. Over the years, Goodman made several trips to Twain's homes in the east. Goodman in his letters and in his visits, advised Twain about his career, advice Twain accepted. In 1868, Goodman helped Mark Twain secure rights to letters Twain had written for the *Alta California*. These letters were the basis for Mark Twain's first book, *The Innocents Abroad*.

Joe Goodman died in San Francisco October 1, 1917. He was seventy-nine. He left a widow and four daughters.

DENNIS E. McCARTHY

Dennis E. McCarthy was twenty when he and Joe Goodman took over the *Territorial Enterprise* in March, 1861. McCarthy was a compositor and printer and was in charge of the pressroom. To his friends he was known as "Mac" or the "Orphan".

McCarthy was born in Melbourne, Australia, February 22, 1850. His parents were not well to do and McCarthy went to work at ten in the pressroms of several San Francisco newspapers. He became the "devil" at the *Evening Journal*, worked his way up to compositor and eventually became a printer working some time for the *Golden Era* where he met Rollin M. Daggett and Joe Goodman, who was three years older.

In January, 1861, he and Goodman left San Francisco for Virginia City where they became partners with Jonathan Williams on the *Enterprise*.

By 1865, Goodman and McCarthy had accumulated small fortunes. McCarthy sold his interest in the *Enterprise*, moved back to San Francisco where he invested heavily in the stock market. Within four months he had lost his fortune. Now married with two children, he returned to Virginia City and reclaimed his job as pressroom foreman.

In the fall of 1866, McCarthy briefly managed Mark Twain's first lecture tour through the mining camps of the Motherlode and Northwestern Nevada.

In 1869, McCarthy, who had bought large shares in Comstock mines when prices were depressed, struck it rich when the Big

Bonanza was discovered and stock prices soared. He moved back to Virginia City where on May 24, 1875 he bought the floundering Virginia Evening *Chronicle*. Within six months McCarthy turned the *Chronicle* into the number one newspaper in Storey County. Within a year the *Chronicle* had the greatest circulation of any newspaper in Nevada.

In 1881, as hard times hit the Comstock, the *Enterprise* and the *Chronicle* consolidated. Always a heavy drinker, McCarthy's drinking grew worse.

Dennis McCarthy died in 1885 and was burried in Lone Mountain Cemetery in Carson City. He was forty-four.

McCarthy, like other men on the *Enterprise*, went to work at an early age and was self-educated. He became one of the most respected newspaper managers and journalists on the Pacific Coast. His writing like his personality was plain, direct, kindly and unpretentious. A friend once said of him, "One of the truest and best men I have ever met." Rollin Daggett, on learning of his death said, "He was a good-hearted, wrong-headed man and I shall miss him when I go to Virginia City."

DAN De QUILLE

Dan De Quille joined the *Enterprise* in the spring of 1862 as the local and mining editor. But for a few absences, De Quille remained with the *Enterprise* for thirty-one years until the paper folded in 1893. During these years, De Quille was one of the most respected and popular writers on the Pacific Coast. He was considered the finest humorist in Virginia City even while Mark Twain wrote for the *Enterprise*.

De Quille was born William Wright, May 9, 1829, in Knox County , Ohio. He was the eldest of nine children born to Paxton and Lucy Wright, Quakers. Paxton Wright was a descendant of Anthony Wright, who sailed from England with William Penn and helped to establish Philadelphia.

In 1849, the Wright family moved to Iowa. There William wrote humorous articles which he submitted to newspapers and magazines. Charles Leeland, editor at *Graham's Magazine*, accepted Wright's articles and encouraged the young writer.

In 1853, Wright married Caroline Coleman who bore five

children. In 1857, he left his family and went west to Nevada where he mined at Omega in Nevada County. For the next several years Wright prospected and mined throughout northwestern Nevada and the western slope of the Sierra Nevada. Under the pen name of Dan De Quille, Wright wrote humorous letters of his exploits to the *Golden Era* where they were published. Though he made little money with his writing, readers looked forward to Dan De Quille's letters. De Quille, slowly established his name as a popular humorist.

In 1859, Wright crossed the Sierra through Yosemite and explored the rich Eastern Sierra mining region near Mono Lake. The Dogtown placers seven miles south of Bridgeport, California had attracted scores of miners and gold had been discovered at nearby Bodie. Twenty years later Bodie would boom and draw many from Virginia City. In 1860, Wright moved on to Silver City in Gold Canyon where he continued prospecting and mining. The *Golden Era* continued publishing his letters; these eventually helped De Quille land a post on the *Enterprise*.

Spring, 1862, Goodman hired De Quille to cover local events and mining news. Possessing a vast firsthand knowledge of mining, De Quille immediately became a respected mining editor whose columns were relied on by miners and speculators. With every new Comstock mining discovery, De Quille was sent to inspect and report his finding. His reports were frank, detailed and reliable. Wright was thereafter known to his friends and the people of Virginia City as Dan or Dandy.

Goodman allowed his writers a free hand. With columns to fill six days a week, *Enterprise* journalists often contributed humorous stories. Through the columns of the *Enterprise*, Dan De Quille became the most widely read of any Western humorist. His humor was gentle and whimsical, sometimes sentimental. A science nut, many of his humorous stories were sort of based on scientific fact or recent discoveries.

De Quille's "solar armor" story is typical of his humor. This story told of a solar armor invention supposed to protect a person from the extreme summer heat. The armor consisted of an India rubber suit, a small air compressor and a battery. De Quille told how the inventor of this solar armor suit started out across Death Valley with the temperture 117 degrees in the shade. A search party

Local Virginia City journalist and friends of Mark Twain. Left to right, William Gillespie, Charles Parker, Dan De Quille, Robert Lowery and Alf. Doten.

found the inventor the next day. Unable to turn the compressor off, the inventor had frozen to death and was found with an eighteen inch icicle stuck to his nose. This, and other De Quille scientific hoaxes, were taken seriously by other journals and were often reprinted, sometimes as far away as Europe. De Quille continually received letters from scientists inquiring about one story or another.

Encouraged by Mark Twain, in 1875 De Quille took a leave of absence from the *Enterprise* and went to Hartford, Connecticut where he lived with Mark Twain and his family while writing *The Big Bonanza*. Twain persuaded his publisher to publish the book. Though *The Big Bonanza* sold well on the West Coast, overall it was a failure. De Quille had hoped *The Big Bonanza* would inable him to leave journalism so he might concentrate on creative writing. In a short time he returned to the *Enterprise*.

In 1893, the *Enterprise* suspended publication. For the next three years De Quille made a bare living by writing articles for the *Salt Lake Transfer* and San Francisco publications. By 1896 his health was broken from years of alcoholism and rheumatism. John Mackay, one of the four silver kings whose Bonanza mines had made Mackay a multi-millionaire, learned of De Quille's condition. A long time friend, Mackay saw that Dan received two of the best suits in town and someone to escort him back to Liberty, Iowa where he lived with his daughter. Mackay gave De Quille his old salary of $60 a week until his death.

Dan De Quille died at Liberty, Iowa March 16, 1898 and was buried in the Oakridge Cemetery.

In part, his obituary read:

William Wright was one of the most gentle, the most amiable, the least worldly-minded of men. He loved the beautiful in all things and seldom spoke of a fault in a friend, never unkindly. He imagined every one as sincere and free from guile as himself...He was a man of no enemies, and his friendships were fervent and sincere. In Virginia City he was loved by everyone; even the children of the hills, the Piutes, knew him as a friend, and if they had a grievance came to him for advice, and he loved them as he loved everything in Nature. Every little flower and living creature was of interest to him. Nevada and her interests he loved with his whole soul, the beauty and grandeur of her mountains and valleys...

Well's Drury said of Dan:

Of all the men I knew on the Comstock I consider Dan De Quille the most thoroughly characteristic of the camp and its inhabitants; in fact, the presiding genius of the Enterprise. *He was a miner before he began to write press, and it was by sending accounts of mining developments in outside camps that he first attracted the attention of the* Enterprise *editors. Through all the years of his reportorial work he never shed his character as a miner. A miner he started out, and a miner he is today--in sprirt if not in deed...All other matters to him appeared inconsequential and of no material interest. If there was a murder, a sensational society episode or a political contest, any one of them was welcome to space after his mining notes were provided for...Dan, was right, judging from his standpoint. He was a miner in a mining country writing for miners, who had a livelier interest in the latest mineral developments...than in learning the result of the Presidential election...*
                    An Editor On The Comstock Lode

Dan De Quille was and remained during Mark Twain's stay, the most popular humorist in Virginia City. He had a great influence on Twain both as a writer and as a friend. Of the two writers, Joe Goodman believed De Quille was destined to become the most successful. Goodman later admitted, though an equal to Mark Twain in talent, De Quille lacked Twain's desire for fame and the skill for marketing his talent.

ROLLIN M. DAGGETT

Rollin M. Daggett was to the *Enterprise* what the armored tank is to the infantry. Stout and heavy, Daggett waddled down Virginia City boardwalks like a bulldog looking for a fight.

Audacious, intelligent, hard drinking, hard living, highly individualistic, Daggett was a man to be taken seriously. With a strong empathy for the trampled and the underdog, Daggett defended justice and right in his editorials. When angered, his words annihilated victims like a chain saw. It was said men went looking for Daggett armed, determined to have satisfaction or Daggett's head. He was not afraid to topple corrupt men in high places. Daggett made enemies but he had many friends.

Rollin Daggett, like Goodman, was a New Yorker, born in Richville, New York, February 22, 1831. His family moved to Ohio where Daggett went to school and learned the printing trade. His father died when he was eleven. At sixteen by himself and with only a rifle, ammunition, salt and a loaf of hard bread, Daggett started on foot across the plains to California. For a while Daggett lived with the Sioux unharmed. The Indians believed Daggett was insane and left him alone though they allowed him to sleep in their wickiups.

After crossing the Rocky Mountains, Daggett joined a wagon train on its way to California. He became friends with a man and his wife and their three children. Cholera, then a deadly threat for emigrants, raged through the wagon train killing many. The man and his wife were stricken. Before the mother died she asked Daggett to deliver her children to friends in Sacramento. Daggett buried the father and mother and fulfilled the mother's dying request.

Through 1850-51, Daggett prospected and mined in the California gold fields eventually earning a sizeable stake. He settled in San Francisco where he found work as a printer.

In December, 1852, Daggett and J. Macdonough Ford published the first issue of the *Golden Era*, the first California literary weekly. The *Golden Era* published news of current events, poetry, fiction, dramatic news, editorials and advertisements. The *Golden Era* actively sought the work of Pacific Coast writers. Bret Harte, Dan De Quille, Joe Goodman and Mark Twain were published in the *Golden Era*.

While Ford took charge of the editorial and publication of the magazine, Daggett hunted for subscribers in the Western Sierra. Within a month Daggett sold 1100 subscriptions in nine mining camps. The *Golden Era* was on its way to having the

Rollin M. Daggett in mid-life. Daggett was associate editor for the *Enterprise* while Mark Twain worked for the paper. Daggett taught Mark Twain to attack wrong doing at every level.

largest circulation of any West Coast publication.

As Daggett roamed through the mining camps, he collected news and stories. These he wrote down and sent to the *Era* under several pen names.

By 1856, the *Golden Era* was the largest California journal in size and circulation.

July, 1860, Daggett left the *Golden Era* to start the *Daily Evening Mirror*. The newspaper failed and Daggett left the paper in January, 1862 and made his way to Virginia City where he opened a brokerage house with a man named Meyers.

About this time he became involved with the *Enterprise* as a journalist and editor. In 1864, Daggett joined the *Enterprise* full time as associate editor. He left the paper in 1874 when Joe Goodman sold the *Enterprise* to William Sharon. Sharon rehired Daggett as editor where, according to Sam Davis, Daggett earned $250 a week, the largest salary of any Nevada newspaperman at that time.

In 1878, Daggett was elected to Congress. He later served as Minister to Hawaii.

During Mark Twain's tenure, Daggett was associate editor. As Joe Goodman invested more time in his poetry and controversial editorials, Daggett took greater control of the paper's content.

Like other *Enterprise* writers, Daggett had wit. It was more pointed than De Quille's and akin to Twain's. One morning Daggett had breakfast with William Sharon. Daggett consumed a huge breakfast when Sharon said, "Heavens, I would give half my fortune for your appetite." "Yes," Daggett answered, "and the other half for my character and lofty bearing."

Daggett's writing style was crisp and clean. Where many writers during this period wrote ornately with great, obscure words and sentences that stretched for miles, Daggett's writing was modern in comparison, unpretentious, unsentimental, to the point with shorter sentences and fewer unnecessary adjectives. This was a highly positive influence on Twain's writing development. For Clemens' early *Enterprise* writings were wordy and forced and they lacked constraint.

Rollin Daggett used satire and his command of language to fight corruption and injustice on any level. His stands were brave; this was a time when men settled their differences with guns and knives. Daggett was a courageous witness to the power of the written word to fight evil and wrong doing. Clemens' writing gradually became more concerned with issues that affected the community as a whole; his satire effectively pointed out incompetence and wrongdoing. This won Clemens the respect of his readers.

Rollin Daggett and Meyers built the Daggett and Meyers building at 25 North B Street. In the fall of 1863, Mark Twain and Dan De Quille shared an apartment on the third floor. Neighbors were Tom Fitch, of the *Virginia Union* and Rollin Daggett.

STEVE GILLIS

Steve Gillis was a printer for the *Enterprise* and later an editor. He was a ninety-five pound tiger who had a knack for getting into brawls. Next to Dan De Quille, Steve Gillis was Mark Twain's closest friend in Virginia City. When Mark Twain left Virginia City, Steve Gillis left with him. Afterward, Steve and Mark roomed together in San Francisco for about six months when Gillis nearly killed a man in a brawl. Twain posted Steve's bail, but when it appeared Gillis' sparing partner would die, Mark and Steve fled San Francisco for brother Jim Gillis' cabin on Jackass Hill. During Twain's stay with Jim Gillis, Mark Twain first heard the famous story of the Calaveras jumping frog. Twain's version catapulted the author into national attention.

Steve Gillis, like Mark Twain, enjoyed playing practical jokes. Twain was often the butt of Gillis' jokes. One of the more well known practical jokes was the time Gillis conspired with other *Enterprise* staffers to rob Mark Twain on the Divide between Gold Hill and Virginia City.

Steve Gillis returned to the *Enterprise* after his trouble in San Francisco. He married the niece of Joe Goodman. Drinking became a problem in later years. Joe Goodman on one occassion wrote Twain about Gillis' "going to the dogs." But Steve Gillis outlived all the *Enterprise* boys. Steve Gillis was eighty when he died April 13, 1918 at Jackass Hill near Sonora.

Other writers employed on the *Enterprise* when Mark Twain worked for the paper were Captain Joe Plunkett, George Dawson, Charles Putnam, Howard P. Taylor and "Lying" Jim Townsend.

The young men of the *Enterprise* helped create the most extraordinary newspaper at that time on the West Coast. Wells Drury wrote of the *Enterprise* years later, "There never has been a paper like the *Enterprise* on the Coast since and never can be again--never one so entirely human, so completely the reflex of a splendid personality and a mining camp's bouyant life."

Rollin Daggett relates an entertaining episode which gives us a glimpse into the high times of those wild *Enterprise* boys during the years Mark Twain was on the paper:

There were many amusing incidents connected with journalism on the Comstock in those days. It was a rough camp and the boys were generally pretty wild fellows.

I remember that Goodman and McCarthy were particularly aggressive, in fact they would fight; fight at the drop of a hat and shoot, too. This was well known to the boys and consequently there was generally a row pending. If news was a little scarce Mark Twain and Dan De Quille, with their fertile brains and active imaginations, could scare up a "story" that would raise the Old Harry, they well knowing that Goodman and McCarthy would back them up.

In 1863 Tom Fitch started a weekly paper in Virginia City called the Accident, *to which Mark Twain has made humorous reference in his "Roughing It." Tom was doing but little at that time, and started the paper more for pastime than anything else. He subsequently became the editor of the Virginia City* Union. *It was not long until from some cause a personal altercation betwee Fitch and Goodman led to a duel. The meeting took place about ten miles from the city, and Fitch received a bullet in his leg. They both stood up manfully, and subsequent explanations made them friends.*

About that time a paper called the Evening Herald *made its appearance in Virginia City. It was edited by H.C. Bennett and it was not long until trouble arose and bitter words passed between the* Enterprise *and the* Herald. *Finally Goodman and McCarthy concluded to put a stop to Bennett's assaults. Arming themselves with revolvers they invaded Bennett's sanctum. The boys from the* Enterprise *followed at a safe distance to see the fun, knowing that Bennett was something on the fight himself.*

Without pausing to exchange courtesies Goodman informed the common enemy that they had come to "clean him out." Very much to their surprise he immediately replied that that was his "best hold," and assuming the offensive he tackled the two without a mo-

ment's hesitation. A rough and tumble fight followed, and the sounds that came from that sanctum were appalling. Every once in a while some of the boys would try to get a peep into the room, but the sound of a pistol shot caused them to return to the friendly protection of a corner. Everybody expected there would be three funerals the next day, but suddenly two forms shot out the door into the street. It took some little time to identify them, but they eventually proved to be Goodman and McCarthy. They went over to the Enterprise *office and washed up, but neither of them could ever give a satisfactory explanation of "how it happened."*

Arrests followed the fight and the trial was a noted one in Virginia City...

These were the men and this was the newspaper Sam Clemens now came to work for.

Sutterly's Photographic Gallery where Mark Twain has pictures of himself taken. *Nevada Historical Society.*

CHAPTER SIX

The Young Sam Clemens

When Sam Clemens arrived in Virginia City, he was twenty-six, to turn twenty-seven November 30. He stood 5 feet, 8½ inches and weighed about 145 pounds. His body was small and slender yet his head seemed almost too large. "His head was striking," Bret Harte wrote. "He had the curly hair, the acquiline nose, and even the acquiline eye--an eye so eagle-like that a second lid would not have surprised me..." Out of this unusual head two piercing eyes dissected the world and the creatures God had placed in it. His eyes were commanding, magnetic, strong yet soft. They caught one's attention, possessed "a calm, penetrating, unwavering gaze," thought George Ade. They seemed wise beyond their years. To William Dean Howells, a lifelong friend, Clemens' eyes were greenish-blue. To Susy Clemens, her father's eyes were blue but to James Fields his eyes were grey. Clemens' eyes likely changed with his moods or with lighting. Dark bushy eyebrows gave his face a serious, meditative appearance. For all his humor, Clemens seldom smiled. This striking head was ornamented with a thick crop of curly, mahogany hair. Clemens in Virginia City at first oiled his hair and combed it back. In time he quit using the oil; his hair grew long and wild and took on the rugged, youthful appearance by which the world later recognized him.

Once he shaved his prospector's beard, his fair skinned face was revealed. It seemed both delicate and rugged, his mouth, "as delicate as a woman's," Kipling wrote. He had not yet grown the thick, bushy moustache which would define his face a lifetime.

Mark Twain in his early thirties. *Nevada Historical Society.*

Though his face conveyed strength and intelligence, his small body at times appeared helpless. It was not the body of a laborer but that of a thinker. Joe Goodman thought Clemens' bodily helplessness belied his great mental capacity. Clemens nearly died as a feeble infant; as an adult he was susceptible to respiratory illnesses, bronchitis, severe colds. His hands were small and delicate, calloused from his mining labors in Aurora.

"His dress was careless, and his general manner one of supreme indifference to surroundings and circumstances," thought Bret Harte. He seemed to some as if he was not all there, that his mind was somewhere else on some other plain normal humans do not visit. It caused him to be absent minded, at times careless in his dress. Howells said, "...he was apt to smile into your face with a subtle but amiable perception, and yet with a sort of remote absence; you were all there for him, but he was not all there for you."

In his mouth at every waking hour was a cigar or pipe. Clemens literally lived in a cloud of tobacco smoke and loved the smell; this was Paradise. He had smoked since a boy and now smoked incessantly. Years later he said of his smoking, "Me, who never learned to smoke, but always smoked; me, who came into this world asking for a light... Why, my old boy, when they used to tell me I would shorten my life ten years by smoking... they little knew how trivial and valueless I would regard a decade that had no smoking in it!" *Enterprise* staffers dubbed his pipe, "The Remains" and "The Pipe of a Thousand Smells."

Clemens moved slowly. To some Clemens appeared lazy. Joe Goodman thought he was, "kind of lazy or slow in his movements." To Rollin Daggett he was "slothful." His strong Missouri drawl inherited from his mother, made Clemens seem that much slower. Susy Clemens said her father lost his drawl in private. Clemens apparently capitalized on his drawl which gave his speech a folksy, down to earth tone.

Clemens readily admitted he hated physical labor. "I do not like to work even when another person does it." Clemens often spoke of himself as being lazy. Once while looking through his Suetonius he found a reference to a Flavius Clemens, a man widely known "for his want of energy." Twain wrote in the margin, "I guess this is where our line starts." Clemens was not lazy; he detested drudgery.

Clemens put his heart and soul into whatever he loved or enjoyed. Once he was commited to a project he worked steadily until the job was completed. He possessed extraordinary tenacity and energy. He spent eight years writing *Huckleberry Finn*; over his lifetime he wrote and rewrote by hand volumes of literature. Though Rollin Daggett said Clemens gave Dan De Quille all the dirty work, De Quille said that he and Clemens agreed to divide the work load. De Quille wrote those items which required attention to detail and numbers. Clemens, on the other hand, was best suited for human interest stories and did not care a lick for items that did not interest him.

One of Clemens' outstanding characteristics was the ease with which he made friends. Clemens was a human magnet and drew people to him naturally. He did not have to work to get the attention of others. Joe Goodman said, "Back in the old days Sam was the best company, the drollest entertainer and the most interesting fellow imaginable. His humor was always cropping out..." Those who knew Clemens best, said his speech was funnier than his writing. Clemens would tell homorous stories for hours while an enraptured gathering laughed till their sides ached and time seemed to pass too quickly. Clemens loved being the center of attention and he was skillful in the ways he acheived it. He was a ham, an actor, a born entertainer. He enjoyed people, enjoyed himself and loved making people laugh and feel good.

His speech was disarmingly frank and unpretentious. He could talk for hours over a wide spectrum of subjects. Conversation stimulated him but he was a better talker than a listener. His speech, especially during the Western years, was often profane. Intimates accepted his profanity, at times wondered at his skill. Katy Leary, Twain's longtime housekeeper said, "It was sort of funny, and part of him some how. Sort of amusing it was--and gay--not like real swearing." Others said Clemens' profane outrages were performances not to be missed. Once in a letter to Howells, Twain attacked an enemy as a "quadrilateral, astronomical, incandescent son-of-a-bitch" and another as a "Damn half-developed feotus!"

Clemens, even during his lectures, spoke in a low, conversational voice but when angered, he lost his drawl, spoke rapidly, and his voice rose in pitch to an acid whine.

Clemens enjoyed playing the mischievious prankster. He often played practical jokes on *Enterprise* friends though he hated practical jokes played on himself. To many, Clemens was a lovable scoundrel whom they easily forgave. Senator William "Bill" Stewart, who knew Clemens well in Virginia City and later in Washington, D.C., said Clemens was, "the most lovable scamp and nuisance who ever blighted Nevada." Clemens while working for the *Enterprise* enjoyed creating news, generally in the form of imaginative stories about people he knew or did not know. Stewart in his *Reminiscences* recalled Clemens the rascal in Virginia City:

> *Sam Clemens was a busy person. He went around putting things in the paper about people, and stirring up trouble. He did not care whether the things he wrote were true or not, just so he could write something, and naturally he was not popular. I did not associate with him.*
>
> *This Clemens one day wrote something about a distinguished citizen of Virginia City, a friend of mine, which was entirely characteristic of Clemens, as it had not the slightest foundation in fact. I remonstrated with him.*
>
> *"You are getting worse every day," I said. "Why can't you be genial, like your brother Orion? You ought to be hung for what you have published this morning."*
>
> *"I don't mean anything by that," returned Clemens. "I do not know this friend of yours. For all I am aware he may be a very desireable and conscientious man. But I must make a living, and so I must write. My employers demand it, and I am helpless..."*
>
> *Clemens had a great habit of making fun of the young fellows and the girls, and wrote ridiculous pieces about parties and other social events, to which he was never invited. After a while he went over to Carson City, and touched up the people over there, and got everybody down on him. I thought he had faded from our midst forever, but the citizens of Carson drove him away. At any rate, he drifted back to Virginia City in a few weeks. He didn't have a friend, but the boys got together and said they would give a party, and invite Clemens to it, and make him feel at home, and respectable and decent, and kindly, and generous, and loving, and considerate of the feelings of others. I could have warned them but I didn't.*
>
> *Clemens went to that party and danced with the prettiest girls,*

and monopolized them, and enjoyed himself, and made a good meal, and then shoved over to the Enterprise *office and wrote the whole thing up in an outrageous manner. He lambasted that party for all the English language would allow, and if any of the guests was unfortunate enough to be awkward or had big feet, or a wart on the nose, Clemens did not forget it. He fairly strained his memory...*

After that he drifted away, and I thought he had been hanged, or elected to Congress, or something like that, and I had forgotten him... I was confident that he would come to no good end, but I have heard of him from time to time since then, and I understand that he has settled down and become respectable.

Stewart and Clemens were good friends. Stewart wrote the above piece years after Twain made fun of him in *Roughing It* and I imagine Stewart, as much a prankster as Clemens, enjoyed his opportunity to get back at Clemens for embarassing him. Clemens was never chased out of Carson City as Stewart wrote. He was highly popular and had many friends. It is true that he wrote items from time to time which embarassed people but they were generally done in jest and the rough humor was appreciated by Comstockers. Of course, if a victim was an enemy, well, he deserved what he got.

Twain approached Stewart in 1867 while writing *The Innocents Abroad*. Twain needed a place to write and a temporary job. Stewart offered Twain his house in Washington, D.C., where Twain lived and wrote *The Innocents Abroad*. Twain worked part-time as Stewart's private secretary, a job he did not relish and which caused kindly Bill Stewart no end of grief.

Twain in, "My Late Senatorial Secretaryship," tells something of the problems Stewart had to deal with:

My employer sent for me one morning tolerably early... There was something portentous in his appearance. His cravat was untied, his hair was in a state of disorder, and his countenance bore about it signs of a suppressed storm. He held a package of letters in his tense grasp, and I knew that the dreaded Pacific mail was in. He said:
"I thought you were worthy of confidence."

I said, "Yes, sir."

He said, "I gave you a letter from certain of my constituents in the State of Nevada, asking the establishment of a post office at Baldwin's Ranch, and told you to answer it, as ingeniously as you could, with arguments which should persuade them that there was no real necessity for an office at that place."

I felt easier. "Oh, if that is all, sir I did do that."

"Yes, you did. I will read your answer for your own humiliation:

" 'Washington, Nov. 24.

Gentlemen: What the mischief do you suppose you want with a post-office at Baldwin's Ranch? It would not do you any good. If any letters came there, you couldn't read them, you know; and, besides, such letters as ought to pass through, with money in them, for other localities, would not be likely to get through, you must perceive at once; and that would make trouble for us all. No, don't bother about a post-office in your camp. I have your best interests at heart, and feel that it would only be ornamental folly. What you want is a nice jail, you know--a nice, substantial jail and a free school. These will be a lasting benefit to you. These will make you really contented and happy. I will move in the matter at once.

Very truly, etc.,
Mark Twain,
For James W.N.**, U.S. Senator.' "

"That is the way you answered that letter. Those people say they will hang me, if I ever enter that district again; and I am perfectly satisfied they will, too."

"Well, sir, I did not know I was doing any harm. I only wanted to convince them."

"Ah. Well, you did convince them, I make no manner of doubt. Now, here is another specimen..."

Clemens enjoyed upsetting and shocking people. This was his idea of fun. Clemens *was* Tom Sawyer, a boy who never grew up. Howells, who knew him extraordinarily well, said, "He was a youth to the end of his days, the heart of a boy with the head of a sage; the heart of a good boy, or a bad boy, but always a wilful boy, and wilfulest to show himself out at every time for just the boy he was."

Clemens remained youthful until his death. He skipped up steps, leap frogged on the floor. He was led by his emotions, always spontaneous, at times impulsive. He defied authority and was wilfully independent. He was eager, always intense, prone to extremes in moods, one moment high and happy, the next, low and depressed. He had extreme reactions of glory and despair, praise and condemnation. He loved pageantry and parades, children and animals, the cat his favorite. Once while staying with Tom Fitch and his family at Washoe City, near Virginia City, Clemens insisted that Jim, the Fitch's Maltese cat, sleep with him every night. He was always raving about one fad or another. He loved bright colors, red, his favorite and later insisted his billiard table have red felt instead of green. He enjoyed pranks and shocking people by outrageous dress. Clemens once showed up at a dance in Gold Hill wearing white pants, huge buffalo shoes and yellow kid gloves. And he enjoyed games, billiards, poker and euchre his favorites in his mining camp days.

When Clemens died at seventy-five, Katy Leary said, "It was a terrible, cruel thing for him to die, really, because he was too young--that is, he felt young, you know, and that made him young..."

Virginia City in the 1870's looking down from Mt. Davidson. The mounds of light colored sand mark the sites of the major mines. Six Mile Canyon is in the upper left corner. *Nevada Historical Society.*

CHAPTER SEVEN

Sam Clemens: *Enterprise Reporter*

Some time during the last two weeks of September, 1862, Clemens finally showed up at the *Enterprise*. The *Enterprise* was then located at 27 North C Street next to the Wells Fargo offices where the Silver Queen Casino stands today. Clemens may have first roomed in the *Enterprise* offices or with a friend. Later he lodged at Mrs. Williamson's, White House boarding house on South C Street. His neighbors were Clement Rice, a reporter for the Virginia *Union*, who became a best friend and William Gillespie, who reported for the *Enterprise* and became first clerk for the Territorial Legislature.

After his hard times at Aurora, Virginia City was more to Clemens' liking. The roaring mining town offered Clemens the same breadth of life as the larger Mississippi River towns he was familiar with and enjoyed. Though Virginia City was not on a waterway and small, it was cosmopolitan and provided Clemens with the variety and wild times he craved. Here were many people from many nations working, living, playing, going about their business. Where life at Aurora was dull and hard, life in Virginia City was easy, exciting and invigorating. At Aurora, Clemens lived in crude shelters and it was always cold. In Virginia City, Clemens had a warm room, 15 restaurants to choose from and more than 50 saloons to drink and socialize in. Clemens was back in the active, social life he enjoyed.

Clemens returned to familiar turf on the *Enterprise*. But for the four and half years as a river pilot, Clemens had worked in printing and newspaper offices since a teenager. The odor of ink, the ticking of the compositors at work, the sound of scribbling quills, the rattling of the printing presses, were all familiar and comfortable and a part of his youth. But now Clemens held a more important position; he created the copy the compositors set and the printing presses manufactured.

Clemens at first felt unsure in his new reporting role. There were times he felt like backing out. But when the thought of unemployment and dependency struck, he decided "necessity is the mother of taking chances."

Sam approached Joe Goodman and asked what he should do. Goodman replied:

...go all over town and ask all sorts of people all sorts of questions, make notes of the information gained, and write them out for publication. And he added:

"Never say 'We learn' so-and so or 'It is reported,' or 'It is rumored,' or 'We understand' so-and so, but go to headquarters and get the absolute facts, and then speak and say 'It is so-and so.' Otherwise, people will not put confidence in your news. Unassailable certainty is the thing that gives a newspaper the firmest and most valuable reputation."

It was the whole thing in a nutshell; and to this day, when I find a reporter commencing his article with "We understand," I gather a suspicion that he has not taken as much pains to inform himself as he ought to have done. I moralize well, but I did not always practice well when I was a city editor; I let fancy get the upper hand of fact too often when there was dearth of news. I can never forget my first day's experience as a reporter. I wandered about town questioning everybody, boring everybody, and finding out that nobody knew anything. At the end of five hours my note-book was still barren. I spoke to Mr. Goodman. He said:

"Dan used to make a good thing out of the haywagons in a dry time when ther were no fires or inquests. Are there no hay-wagons in from Truckee? If there are, you might speak of the renewed activity and all that sort of thing, in the hay business, you know. It isn't sensational or exciting, but it fills up and looks business-like."

I canvassed the city again and found one wretched old hay-truck dragging in from the country. But I made affluent use of it. I multiplied it by sixteen, brought it into town from sixteen different directions, made sixteen separate items of it, and got up such another sweat about hay as Virginia City had never seen in the world before.

This was encouraging. Two nonpareil colums had to be filled, and I was getting along. Presently, when things began to look dismal again, a desperado killed a man in a saloon and joy returned once more. I never was so glad over any mere trifle before in my life. I said to the murderer:

"Sir, you are a stranger to me, but you have done me a kindness this day which I can never forget. If whole years of gratitude can be to you any slight compensation, they shall be yours. I was in trouble and you have relieved me nobly and at a time when all seemed dark and drear. Count me your friend from this time forth, for I am not a man to forget a favor."

If I did not really say that to him I at least felt a sort of itching desire to do it. I wrote up the murder with a hungry attention to details, and when it was finished experienced but one regret-- namely, that they had not hanged my benefactor on the spot, so that I could work him up too.

Next I discovered some emigrant wagons going into camp on the plaza and I found that they had lately come through the hostile Indian country and had fared rather roughly. I made the best of the item that the circumstances permitted, and felt that if I were not confined with rigid limits by the presence of the reporters of the other papers I could add particulars that would make the article much more interesting. However, I found one wagon that was going to California, and made some judicious inquiries of the proprietor. When I learned, through his short and surly answers to my cross-questioning, that he was certainly going on and would not be in the city next day to make trouble, I got ahead of the other papers, for I took down his list of names and added his party to the killed and wounded. Having more scope here, I put this wagon through an Indian fight that to this day has no parallel in history.

My two columns were filled. When I read them over in the morning I felt that I had found my legitimate occupation at last. I reasoned within myself that news, and stirring news, too, was what a paper needed, and I felt that I was peculiarly endowed with the ability to furnish it. Mr. Goodman said that I was as good a reporter as Dan. I desired no higher commendation. With encouragement like that, I felt I could take my pen and murder all the immigrants on the plains if need be, and the interests of the paper demanded it.

Roughing It

Whether or not Clemens put the emigrants through an "Indian fight that to this day has no parallel in history," we cannot be certain. Only a scattering of early *Enterprise* issues survive; this article is not among existing issues. It is true, while reporting for the *Enterprise*, Clemens exaggerated events to make his articles more entertaining. He, Bill Stewart and others testify to his skill of avoiding facts.

However, one of Clemens' first hoaxes written for the *Enterprise* has survived, the "Petrified Man", published October 4. With the seriousness of Job, Clemens told unsuspecting readers of a petrified man discovered at Gravelly Ford near the Humboldt Mining District about 200 miles northeast of Virginia City. In part it read:

Every limb and feature of the stone mummy was perfect, not even excepting the left leg, which had evidently been a wooden one during the lifetime of the owner--which lifetime, by the way, came to a close about a century ago, in the opinion of a savant who has examined the defunct. The body was in a sitting posture, and leaning against a huge mass of croppings; the attitude was pensive, the right thumb rested against the side of the nose; the left thumb partially supported the chin, the forefinger pressing the inner corner of the eye, and drawing it partly open; the right eye was closed, and the fingers of the right hand spread out. This strange freak of nature created a profound sensation in the vicinity.

Clemens added that a coroner's inquest superintended by "Justice Sewell or Sowell" concluded the "deceased came to his death from protracted exposure." When citizens offered to give the body a decent burial by blasting the man from his limestone seat, the Judge declared that the desecration would be "little less than sacrilege."

1925

Mark Twain's writing desk, *Territorial Enterprise* offices, Virginia City, Nevada. *Nevada Historical Society.*

Not content to allow the article to do its damage, the following day, Clemens pressed the hoax further:

Mr. Herr Weisnicht has just arrived in Virginia City from the Humboldt mines and regions beyond. He brings with him the head and foot of the petrified man, lately found in the mountains near Gravelly Ford. A skillful assayer has analyzed a small portion of the dirt found under the nail of the great toe and pronounces the man to have been a native of the Kingdom of New Jersey. As a trace of "speculation" is still discernible in the left eye, it is thought the man was on his way to what is now the Washoe mining region [Northwestern Nevada] for the purpose of locating the Comstock. The remains brought in are to be seen in a neat glass case in the third story of the Library Building, where they have been temporarily placed by Mr. Weisnicht for the inspection of the curious, and where they may be examined by any one who will take the trouble to visit them.

Mark Twain, years later explained why he wrote the "Petrified M a n : ''

...In the fall of 1862, in Nevada and California, the people got to running wild about extraordinary petrifications and other natural marvels... This mania was becoming a little ridiculous... I felt called upon to destroy this growing evil...

I had a temporary falling out with Mr. _____, the new coroner and justice of the peace of Humboldt, and thought I might as well touch him up a little at the same time and make him ridiculous, and thus combine pleasure with business. So I told, in patient belief-compelling detail, all about the finding of a petrified man at Gravelly Ford (exactly a hundred and twenty miles... from where _____ lived); how all the savants of the immediate neighborhood had been to examine it... how those savants all pronounced the petrified man to have been in a state of complete petrification for over ten generations; and then, with a seriousness that I ought to have been ashamed to assume, I stated that as soon as Mr. _____ heard the news he summoned a jury, mounted his mule, and posted off, with noble reverence for official duty, on that awful five days journey, through alkali, sagebrush, peril of body, and imminent starvation, to hold and inquest *on this man that had been dead and turned to everlasting stone for more than three hundred years!...*

From beginning to end the "Petrified Man" squib was a string of roaring absurdities, albeit they were told with an unfair pretense of truth that even... I was in some danger of believing my own fraud. But I really had no desire to deceive anybody, and no expectation of doing it... But I was too ingenious...

As a satire on the petrification mania... my Petrified Man was a disheartening failure; for everybody received him in innocent good faith...

Sketches New and Old

The "Petrified Man" was reprinted by other Western papers. Most readers accepted the article as fact. The story later appeared in the London *Lancet*, a serious journal of medicine and news.

Clemens intended the "Petrified Man" to embarass Coroner Sewall of Humboldt mining district with whom Clemens was angry. Sewall had apparently refused to forward details regarding recent deaths. Clemens succeeded in embarassing Sewall who reportedly received hundreds of inquiries about the mysterious petrified man. Clemens, true to his nature, had gotten revenge, "I could not have gotten more real comfort out of him without killing him," Mark Twain later wrote.

The "Petrified Man" was the first Western article Clemens used to satirize human stupidity. And, the first of many articles Clemens wrote to embarass men with whom he was at odds or whose motives he disapproved.

Sam Clemens became a sort of middle child on the *Enterprise* staff; there were men older and younger. Dennis McCarthy at twenty-one was the youngest. Joe Goodman and Steve Gillis were twenty-four. Clemens at twenty-six was in the middle. Rollin Daggett was thirty-one and Dan De Quille was the senior at 33.

The *Enterprise* staff was a close fraternity of intelligent, young bachelors, except for Dan De Quille, who was married but whose family lived in Iowa. The men worked and played together. After the paper went to press at two in the morning, the staff and the compositors gathered in the composing room, drank beer and sang the popular war songs of the day until dawn.

Clemens' life fell into a routine. He stayed up late, often until dawn, went to bed in the early morning hours waking around eleven or twelve. After a large breakfast of steak and eggs, lots of coffee, pie or cake, he roamed the town spending much time in the saloons where men gathered and news was easy to find. If there was a new strike in one of the mines, he along with Dan De Quille, the chief mining reporter, went to inspect. There were frequent murders and fights and while reporting on one, another would break out not far away. There were the usual trips to the police station to gather details of recent crimes. The local stock exchange was a good place to find news; it was always busy and something exciting was always happening.

The life of a roaming reporter suited Clemens perfectly. He enjoyed mixing with people; he was interested in learning what others knew. He was full of nervous energy and enjoyed movement though trudging up and down Virginia City's steep streets probably became a chore. As time passed, Clemens became more of a local columnist than news reporter. In such a close knit community as Virginia City, Clemens' magnetic personality was noticed. As a member of the *Enterprise* staff, he was one of a select elite. There were free passes to shows, complimentary drinks and free dinners for plugging local businesses in his column. In return for mentioning their mines in the *Enterprise*, mine owners gave Clemens hundreds of dollars in free mining stocks; some useless, some quite valuable which Clemens traded or sold. Clemens earned twenty five dollars a week, an excellent salary at that time, five dollars a week more than miners made risking their necks in dangerous mines. With so much given to him plus his high salary, Clemens was living high after his penny pinching days at Aurora.

Clemens spent late afternoons and evenings writing at the long table in the *Enterprise* offices. When he finished an article, Dan read it over or Clemens passed it to Rollin Daggett, the assistant editor. When an article was approved, Clemens handed it to the compositor who hand set each word with individual metal letters in large wooden cases used to print the newspaper.

Dan De Quille, then the local reporter and editor, stayed with the paper until mid-November teaching Clemens the ropes. Goodman hired Clemens to replace De Quille who was taking a leave of absence in order to visit his wife and family in Iowa. De Quille would not return to Virginia City and the *Enterprise* until the end of July, 1863.

Virginia City was then a twenty-four hour town. After the paper was put to bed, the *Enterprise* boys frequented their favorite saloons and restaurants. Some of their favorite saloons were John Piper's Old Corner Saloon in the basement of his Opera House at the corner of B and Union, Tom Peaseley's Sazerac at 10 South C Street near Union, Almack's, The International Hotel, The Delta and when Maguire's Opera House opened, the boys met at the Branch Saloon. Favorite restaurants were the Chauvel House Restaurant at 12 North C Street, Delmonico's at 32 and 34 South C Street between Union and Taylor, the Eagle Restaurant and Barnum's at the corner of B and Sutton. For entertainment there were shows at Piper's Opera House, later Maguire's; there were dance hall's and hurdy gurdy girls and of course, many prostitutes. Though De Quille and other journalists visited the redlight districts, there is no evidence Clemens did. Clemens, a billiards nut, probably spent considerable time at the Bank Exchange Billiard Saloon at 5 North B Street.

When Dan De Quille left in November, Clemens was on his own as the local reporter and editor. The ink had barely dried on De Quille's pen before Clemens was joking in his columns about Dan's leaving. Dan, said Clemens, had gone East to recuperate from the strain of:

> *...creating big strikes in the mines and keeping all the mills in this district going, whether their owners were willing or not. These herculean labors greatly undermined his health, but he went bravely on, and we are proud to say that as far as these things were concerned, he never gave up--the miners never did, and never could have conquered him. He fell, under the scarcity of pack-trains and hay-wagons. These had been the bulwark of the local column; his confidence in them was like unto that men have in four aces; murders, forgeries, fires, distinguished arrivals, were creatures of chance, which might or might not occur at any moment... when these failed last week, he said "Et tu Brute" and gave us his pen. His constitution suddenly warped, split and went under, and Daniel succumbed. We have a saving hope, though, that his trip across the Plains through 1,800 miles of cheerful hay-stacks, will so restore*

our loved and lost to his ancient health and energy, that when he returns next fall he will be able to run our five hundred mills as easily as he used to keep five-score running.

In the lower northeast end of Virginia City was Chinatown where about a thousand Chinese lived. Usually peaceable, occassionally there was trouble. Apparently a Chinaman was murdered, the suspect captured and a trial begun. Clemens observed the trial. In a piece called "The China Trial," you can see how Clemens used an ordinary murder trial to entertain readers. By exaggerating details, Clemens turned the serious event into a hilarious spectacle. In part he wrote:

...We were there, yesterday, not because we were obliged to go, but just because we wanted to. The more we see of this aggravated trial, the more profound does our admiration for it become. It commenced as an assassination, the assassinated man neglected to die, and they turned it into assault and battery; after this the victim did die, whereupon his murderers were arrested and tried for perjury; they convicted one Chinaman, but when they found out it was the wrong one, they let him go--and why they should have been so almighty particular is beyond our comprehension; then, in the afternoon, the officers went down and arrested Chinatown again for the same old offense, and put it in jail--but what shape the charge will take this time no man can foresee: the chances are that it will be about a standoff between arson and robbing the mail. Capt. White hopes to get the murderers of the Chinaman hung one of these days, and so do we, for that matter, but we do not expect anything of the kind. You see, these Chinamen are all alike, and they cannot identify each other. They mean well enough, and they really show a disinterested anxiety to get some of their friends and relatives hung, but the same misfortune overtakes them every time: they make mistakes and get the wrong man, with unvarying accurancy. With a zeal in behalf of justice which cannot be to highly praised, the whole Chinese population have accused each other of this murder, each in his regular turn, but fate is against them. They ·cannot tell each other apart. There is only one way to manage this thing with strict equity: hang the gentle Chinese promiscuously until justice is satisfied.

In this article, Clemens again used exaggeration to point out the idiocies of human affairs. Clemens perfected this technique while in the West and made strong use of it in his first two books, *The Innocents Abroad* and *Roughing It*.

In the fall, the Washoe Zephyrs begin, fierce winds from the west that roar down Mt. Davidson and wreak havoc in town. Washoe Zephyrs have been known to topple houses and tear off roofs. Clemens noted the Zephyr phenomenon and commented in his column how a recent Washoe Zephyr tore through town

> *...picked up a shooting gallery, two lodging houses and a drug store from their tall wooden stilts and set them down again some ten or twelve feet back of their original location, with such a degree of roughness as to jostle their insides into a sort of chaos... There were many guests in the lodging houses at the time of the accident, but it is pleasant to reflect that they seized their carpet sacks and vacated the premises with an alacrity suited to the occasion.*

Clemens was in best form writing human interest stories where he was free to interpret events in his own humorous way. He enjoyed writing about people and he was aware that people liked reading about other people. He did not enjoy reporting which required him to carefully note numbers, measurements and solid facts and made no attempt to hide his preference. Once while describing the assaying process, he went along fairly well until the end when he apologized for half-remembering some of the process "owing to lager beer." He concluded the article with:

> *...Science is a very pleasant subject to dilate upon, and we consider that we are as able to dilate upon it as any man that walks-- but if we have been guilty of carelessness in any part of this article, so that our method of assaying as set forth herein may chance to differ from Mr. Theall's, we would advise that gentleman to stick to his own plan nevertheless, and not go to following ours--his is as good as any known to science. If we have struck anything new in our method, however, we shall be happy to hear of it, so that we can take steps to secure ourself the benefits acruing therefrom.*

In mid-November, Joe Goodman sent Clemens to Carson City to

report on the second Territorial Legislature which met mid-November through December. Sam stayed in Carson City at Orion's house with his brother, his wife, Mollie and their seven year old daughter, Jennie. This house still stands and is located at the northwest corner of Spear and Division streets at 502 N. Division.

Orion Clemens as Secretary of Nevada Territory, was second in command to Govenor Nye. Orion was acting governor when Nye was out of the Territory which was frequently. As brother to the acting Governor and legislative reporter for the most powerful voice in the Territory, Clemens was someone to be reckoned with. Though politics and bureaucratic shuffling bored Clemens to death, he enjoyed making fun of politicians who took themselves too serioulsy and legislative bills that made no sense.

For six weeks, Clemens attended the daily legislative meetings at the Warm Springs Hotel, today the Nevada State Penitentiary on east Fifth Street. Abe Curry had kindly donated his hotel as a place for legislators to meet.

After legislative meetings, reporters and representatives met in the Carson saloons.

Clement Rice, Clemens' boarding house neighbor and reporter for the Virginia *Union*, also attended the legislative meetings. Rice was an experienced legislative reporter. After reading one of Clemens' reports in the *Enterprise*, Rice published a column ridiculing Clemens' political naivete. Clemens bounced back with a stunning rebuttal calling Rice's reports unreliable. This began a series of editorial battles between Clemens and Rice. The attacks were made in fun; Clemens and Rice were good friends and later traveled to San Francisco together. The bantering at times was hilarious. Clemens repeatedly referred to Rice as the "Unreliable" and the name stuck. Clemens depicted the Unreliable as a seedy drunk who was forever borrowing money for drinks. Western newspapers followed the bantering between the rival reporters with great interest. On one occasion Clemens wrote of the Unreliable:

...This poor miserable outcast, crowded himself into the Firemen's Ball night before last, and glared upon the happy scene with his evil eye for few minutes. He had his coat buttoned up to his

chin, which is the way he always does when he has no shirt on. As soon as the management found out he was there, they put him out, of course. They had better have allowed him to stay, though, for he walked straight across the street, with all his vicious soul aroused, and climbed in at the back window of the supper room and gobbled up the last crumb of the repast provided for the guests, before he was discovered. This accounts for the scarcity of provisions at the Firemen's supper that night. Then he went home and wrote a particular description of our ball costume with his ususal meanness, as if such information could be of any consequence to the public. He never vouchsafed a single compliment to our dress, either, after all the care and taste we had bestowed upon it. We despise that man.

On another occasion Clemens wrote an obituary for the Unreliable. The Unreliable, he wrote,

became a newspaper reporter, and crushed Truth to earth and kept her there; he bought and sold his own notes, and never paid his board; he pretended great friendship for Gillespie [clerk of the first Territorial Legislature] in order to get to sleep with him; then he took advantage of his bed fellow and robbed him of his glass eye and false teeth; of course he sold the articles, and Gillespie was obliged to issue more county scrip than the law allowed, in order to get them back again; the Unreliable broke into my trunk at Washoe City, and took jewelry and fine clothes and things, worth thousands and thousands of dollars; he was present, without invitation at every party and ball and wedding which transpired in Carson during thirteen years... He is dead and buried now, though, let him rest, let him rot...

P.S. By private letters from Carson, since the above was in type, I am pained to learn that the Unreliable, true to his unnatural instincts, came to life again in the midst of his funeral sermon, and remains so to this moment. He was always unreliable in life--he could not even be depended upon in death. The shrouded corpse shoved the coffin lid to one side, rose to a sitting position, cocked his eye at the minister and smiling said, "O let up... loan me two bits!" The frightened congregation rushed from the house, and the Unreliable followed them, with his coffin on his shoulder. He sold it for two *dollars and a half, and got drunk at a "bit house" [low class saloon] on the proceeds. He is still drunk.*

In early January, 1863, Clemens returned to Virginia City and took up his old position as the local reporter. While attending an Odd Fellows ball at Gold Hill, January 7, someone stole his hat. Clemens in pretended concern for the thief published a warning:

> *We have been suffering from the seven years' itch for many months. It is probably the most aggravating disease in the world. It is contagious. That man has commenced a career of suffering which is frightful to contemplate; there is no cure for the distemper--it must run its course; there is no respite for its victim, and but little alleviation of its torments to be hoped for; the unfortunate's only resource is to bathe in sulphur and molasses and let his finger nails grow. Further advice is unnecessary--instinct will prompt him to scratch.*

Up to this time, all Clemens' *Enterprise* articles were published without a by-line. Now Clemens wanted notoriety and he had come up with a way to achieve it.

Abe Curry's, Warm Springs Hotel, where the early Territorial Legislatures met and where Mark Twain reported. Today this is part of the Nevada State Penitentiary on east Fifth Street. *Nevada Historical Society.*

Clement Rice, the "Unreliable," reporter for the Virginia *Union* and a good friend of Mark Twain's. *Special Collections, University of Nevada, Reno.*

James Nye, Territorial Governor of Nevada, the shrewd politician who became one of Nevada's first Senators. Mark Twain gave Nye considerable space in, *Roughing It.*

This is believed to be the saloon of the Ormsby House Hotel where Mark Twain and members of the Third House met after legislative meetings. *Nevada Historical Society.*

Orion Clemens' home today in Carson City. Here Mark Twain lived with Orion, Mollie and Jennie Clemens when reporting in Carson City. *Larry Tanner photo.*

Bill Stewart's home in Carson City at the northwest corner of King and Minnesota Streets. Governor James Nye bought the house in 1864. Mark Twain no doubt visited the house often when in Carson. *Larry Tanner photo.*

CHAPTER EIGHT

Sam Clemens Becomes Mark Twain

February 16, 1863, Clemens wrote his mother and sister from Virginia City:

> *They [Goodman and the* Enterprise *staff] let me go, about the first of the month, to stay twenty-four hours in Carson, and I stayed a week. Perhaps they haven't much confidence in me now. If they have, I am proud to say it is misplaced. I am very well satisfied here. They pay me six dollars a day, and I make 50 percent profit by only doing three dollars' worth of work.*

Surprisingly, Clemens did not tell his mother and sister about his new pen name. On January 31, Clemens wrote a dispatch from Carson City and signed it, "Mark Twain". It was the first time Clemens used the pen name as a by-line. The article was published in the *Enterprise* several days later. The article was not extraordinary and there was no fanfare. Mark Twain was born quietly.

Clemens had an official version of how he conjured his famous pen name. He told the story thousands of times during his long career. It was published in his autobiography and in a letter to the *Daily Alta California* published June 9, 1877:

Dear Sir:

"Mark Twain" was the nom de plume of one Captain Isaiah

Sellers, who used to write river news over it for the New Olreans Picayune. *He died in 1863 and as he could no longer need that signature, I laid violent hands upon it without asking permission of the proprietor's remains. That is the history of the nom de plume I bear.*

Yours,
Samuel L. Clemens

Isaiah Sellers did write river news for the *Picayune* but he never used the pen name, "Mark Twain." Scholars have examined Sellers personal journals; they found no reference to "Mark Twain". Furthermore, Sellers was still alive when Clemens first called himself "Mark Twain".

A more credible version, is based on Mark Twain's drinking habits while he lived in Virginia City. This version would have embarrased Mark Twain, later the successful author and Eastern socialite; it is understandable why he prefered the Sellers story.

In Virginia City, Mark Twain's drinking and hell raising were well known. There is evidence to substantiate this claim. Here are just a few published items:

The Virginia *Evening Bulletin* told of a loose sheep to which "...Sam Clemens has imparted... something of his own fondness for whisky, and we expect every day to hear of his being arrested for swearing and insulting ladies in the street," (July 10, 1863). The next day the *Bulletin* reported that they had

> *...found Jack Perry's Deputy, Mark Twain, expostulating with a newly arrested subject, who insisted that Mark Twain had stolen his gin bottle and boots. We don't believe the latter accusation, but for the former--there was a bottle in Mark's pocket in lieu of the one he gave us, and he told us significantly when making the gift, that he was going "prospecting" for another."*

The Gold Hill *News* reported,

> *...Mark Twain, Jim Hardy, Judge Leconey, See-Yup, and a lot of other Chinamen at Virginia, are having a series of "high old" drunks, making as an excuse for their debauchery, the presenta-*

tion of "Stars" to Policemen. This thing will probably go, unless, Hirshman shuts down on them, or until the whole present police force is applied. We are not going to interfere with their innocent amusement...

October 26, 1863

Before leaving for Lake Tahoe for a brief respite, Mark Twain wrote in the *Enterprise*, "I take with me a broken spirit, blighted hopes and a busted constitution. Also some gin." The next day he wrote that he had adjourned the Third House convention because it was time for him to take his, "regular gin and molasses."

Alf Doten in his journal told of Mark Twain's visit to Como, a mining camp east of Carson City high in the Pine Nut Mountains. Twain had been sent by Goodman to inspect the mines and make a report. But Twain was more interested in the local brewery. Doten queried him about this:

> *"Mark, you don't seem to get out among the mines and write 'em up. If you'll come along with me to the top of the hill I'll point you out all the quartz ledges in the district, give you the names of the mines, and the aggravating particulars, just as good as if you tramped all around among them yourself. Splendid view, Mark; come along up and I'll give you the whole thing."*
>
> *"...Say, Alf, do you know who you remind me of?"*
>
> *"Well, no, Mark, I don't know as I do,"...*
>
> *"Well, you remind me of that fellow we read of in the Bible, called the devil, who took the Savior up on top of a high mountain, where he could see all over the world and offered to give him the whole thing if he would fall down and worship him. Only you ain't the devil and I ain't the Savior, by a blamed sight. How far do you say it is up there? Only half a mile? Well, no, thank you all the same, but I'm too derned lazy. Let's go down to the brewery."*
>
> *Journals of Alfred Doten*

Twain led Doten into the brewery each morning for three days where they stayed and drank all day. Of Como, Twain reported in the *Enterprise*,

This new mining town, with its romantic name is one of the best

populated and most promising camps, but as to the mines, I have started out several times to inspect them, but never could get past the brewery.

There is the famous story of Artemus Ward and Mark Twain's one week binge; more on this later.

Twain's Western booze habit was probably best noted by Rev. Horatio Stebbins, a San Franciscan friend. When Mark Twain's future father-in-law wrote Stebbins and inquired as to what kind of man Mark Twain was, Stebbins pointedly wrote back that Twain would, "fill a drunkard's grave."

In Virginia City, Mark Twain, Dan De Quille, Steve Gillis, Dennis McCarthy, Rollin Daggett and other *Enterprise* staffers formed a group called the "Companion's of the Jug." At Goodman's request they changed the name to the "Visigoths." The Visigoths met, among other places, in a beer saloon in the basement of the *Enterprise* building which fronted on D Street. According to Rollin Daggett, the daily allowance for the boys was a, "ten gallon keg, which was always consumed before the paper went to press. Mark Twain was amoung the regular attendants, and consumed his portion of the daily allowance with the most astonishing regularity, although he seldom indulged in anything more intoxicating than beer." It would seem from this comment, that the *Enterprise* staff likely took beer instead of coffee breaks which would not have been uncommon in Virginia City at this time. In the D Street beer saloon and other saloons, the boys met with friends and visiting celebrities.

Stories like these lead to a more credible version as to how Clemens created his famous pen name. George W. Cassidy, a journalist who knew Clemens in Virginia City, said the name originated in John Piper's bar, the Old Corner Saloon.

We knew Clemens in the early days and know exactly how he became to be dubbed "Mark Twain". John Piper's saloon on B Street used to be the grand rendevous for all the Virginia City Bohemians. Piper conducted a cash business and refused to keep any books. As a special favor, however, he would occasionally chalk down drinks to the boys, on the wall back of the bar. Sam Clemens, when localizing for the Enterprise, *always had an account, with the balance against him on Piper's wall. Clemens was by no means a Coal Oil Tommy--he drank for the pure and unadulterated love of the ardent. Most of his drinking was conducted in single-handed contests, but ocasionally he would invite Dan De Quille, Charley Parker, Bob Lowery, or Alf Doten never more than one of them, however, at a time, and whenever he did, his invarible parting injunction to Piper was to "Mark Twain", meaning two chalkmarks, of course.*

It is easy to imagine Sam Clemens in the Virginia City saloons, his language still full of the river jargon he had used daily for four and a half years, asking the barkeep to "mark twain"--place two drinks on his tab. Fellow reporters must have quickly picked up this expression and nicknamed Clemens, "Mark Twain." Friends were calling Clemens "Mark" before Clemens signed the name to his January 31 dispatch.

John Piper, who operated Piper's Opera House and the Old Corner Saloon where Sam Clemens and others drank. *Special Collections, University of Neveda, Reno.*

After Mark Twain established himself in elite Eastern social circles, he coveted his social position. His early wild, boozing years were an embarassment and he publicly denied the stories of his Western drinking. When he married Olivia Langdon, he tried to straighten himself out for her sake. Having lived on the river and in the mining camps, Clemens had known the coarser side of life and he was wise enough to realize the effect booze could have on his writing and career. Years later he wrote, "I love a drink, but I never encourage drunkeness by harping on its alleged funny side."

Mark Twain's *Enterprise* cronies were not so fortunate. Dennis McCarthy died of alcoholism at 44. Steve Gillis became an alcoholic; Dan De Quille battled booze for years and it wrecked his health.

It is important to look at Twain's Virginia City drinking in context. There were saloons every ten feet along C Street. Saloons

Piper's Opera House, the third version, built after the second opera house was burned in 1883. Piper's Old Corner Saloon was located here where Sam Clemens was first called Mark Twain. Mark and Dan De Quille lived about 100 yards north of here. *Larry Tanner Photo.*

were important places to gather news and socialize. There was little entertainment and the mining town was isolated. The local water tasted awful and was full of arsenic. Mark Twain and the *Enterprise* boys were young and Virginia City was one big twenty-four hour party. Twain would have been more than mortal not to drink.

Alcohol is still a part of Virginia City and Nevada. A Virginia City bartender told the author, "You can tell who the town drunks are by the splinters in their hands," referring to the wooden board-walks and the way local drunks find their way home. In one saloon a modern day "Companion of the Jug" said, "Now that I'm an alcoholic, I'm an acrobat and can walk on my hands," then he dropped to the floor and crawled on all fours.

That's Virginia City humor.

Inside Piper's Opera House. The original Opera House probably looked similar to this. Here Mark Twain gave some of his first lectures. *Nevada Historical Society.*

CHAPTER NINE

Wild Times in Virginia City

In the early months of 1863, Virginia City exploded in a speculation frenzy. Several rich strikes caused a furor; the stock market went through the roof; thousands made their way to Virginia City by stage, by horseback and on foot. Tiny Virginia City now had 15-18,000 crazed citizens roaming its steep streets. The saloons, restaurants, gambling houses, brothels, dance halls, were jammed day and night. Virginia City had become a twenty-four hour wide open, hard living, mining town and nearly every aspect of human life could be observed in a twenty-four hour period.

Mark Twain in *Roughing It*, paints Virginia City as he knew it during the flush times:

> *Six months after my entry into journalism the grand "flush times" of Silverland began, and continued with unabated splendor for three years. All difficulty about filling up the "local department" ceased, and the only trouble now was how to make the lengthened columns hold the world of incidents and happenings that came to our literary net every day. Virginia had grown to be the "livest" town for its age and population. The sidewalks swarmed with people-- to such an extent, indeed, that it was literally no easy matter to stem the human tide. The streets themselves were just as crowded with quartz-wagons, freight teams,and other vehicles. The procession was endless. So great was the pack, that buggies frequently had to wait half an hour for an opportunity to cross the principal street. Joy sat on every countenance, and there was a*

glad, almost fierce, intensity in every eye, that told of the money-getting schemes that were seething in every brain and the high hope that held sway in every heart. Money was as plenty as dust; every individual considered himself wealthy, and a melancholy countenance was nowhere to be seen. There were military companies, fire companies, brass bands, banks, hotels, theaters, "hurdy-gurdy houses," wide-open gambling palaces, political pow-wows, civic processions, street fights, murders, inquests, riots, a whisky-mill every fifteen steps, a Board of Aldermen, a Mayor, a City Surveyor, a City Engineer, a Chief of the Fire Department, with First, Second and Third Assistants, a Chief of Police, City Marshal, and a large police force, two Boards of Mining Brokers, a dozen breweries, and half a dozen jails and station-houses in full operation, and some talk of building a church. The "flush times" were in magnificent flower! Large fire-proof brick buildings were going up in the principal streets, and the wooden suburbs were spreading out in all directions. Town lots soared up to prices that were amazing.

The great "Comstock lode" stretched its opulent length straight through the town from north to south, and every mine on it was in diligent process of development. One of these mines alone employed six hundred and seventy-five men, and in the matter of elections the adage was, "as the 'Gould and Curry' goes, so goes the city." Laboring-men's wages were four and six dollars a day, and they worked in three "shifts" or gangs, and the blasting and picking and shoveling went on without ceasing, night and day.

The "city"... claimed a population of fifteen thousand to eighteen thousand, and all day long half of this little army swarmed the streets like bees and the other half swarmed among the drifts and tunnels of the "Comstock," hundreds of feet down in the earth directly under those same streets. Often we felt our chairs jar, and heard the faint boom of a blast down in the bowels of the earth under the office.

...The city and all the great mountainside were riddled with mining-shafts. There were more mines than miners. True, not ten of these mines were yielding rock worth hauling to a mill, but everybody said, "Wait till the shaft gets down where the ledge comes in solid, and then you will see!" So nobody was discouraged. These were nearly all "wildcat" mines, and wholly worthless, but *nobody believed it then. The "Ophir," the "Gould and Curry", the "Mexican," and other great mines on the Comstock lead in Virginia and Gold Hill were turning out huge piles of rich rock every day, and every man believed that his little wildcat claim was as good as any on the "main lead" and would infallibly be worth a thousand dollars a foot when he "got down where it came in solid"...So the thousand wildcat shafts burrowed deeper and deeper into the earth day by day, and all men were beside themselves with hope and happiness. How they labored, prophesied, exulted!...Every one of these wildcat mines--not mines, but holes in the ground over imaginary mines--was incorporated and had handsomely engraved "stock" and the stock was salable, too. It was bought and sold with feverish avidity on the boards every day. You could go up on the mountainside, scratch around and find a ledge (there was no lack of them), put up a "notice" with a grandiloquent name on it, start a shaft, get your stock printed, and with nothing whatever to prove that your mine was worth a straw, you could put your stock on the market and sell out for hundreds and even thousands of dollars. To make money, and make it fast, was as easy as it was to eat your dinner. Every man owned "feet" in fifty different wildcat mines and considered his fortune made. Think of a city with not one solitary poor man in it!...They burrowed away, bought and sold, and were happy.*

Mark Twain, a risk taker and gambler at heart, gambled, traded and sold mining stock like the rest of Virginia City's crazed citizens. At one point he claimed he had a whole trunk full of mining stock, some of it worthless, some valuable.

February 16, 1863, he wrote his mother and sister:

Well, I have no news to report, unless it will interest you to know that they "struck it rich" in the "Burnside" ledge last night. The stock was worth ten dollars a foot this morning. It sells at a hundred tonight. I don't own in it, Madam, though I might have owned several hundred feet of it yesterday, you know, and I assure you I would, if I had known they were going to "strike it". None of us are prophets, though. However, I take an absorbing delight in the stock market. I love to watch the prices go up. My time will come after a while, and then I'll rob somebody. I pick up a foot or two oc-

casionally for lying about somebody's mine. I shall sell out one of these days, when I catch a susceptible emigrant. If Orion writes you a crazy letter about the "Emma Gold and Silver Mining Company," pay no attention to it. It is rich, but he owns very little stock in it. If he gets an eighth share in the adjoining company, though let him blow. It will be all right. He may never get it, however.

Years later he wrote of his mining investments:

I entered upon a affluent career in Virginia City, and by a judicious investment of labor and the capital of friends, became the owner of about all the worthless wildcat mines there were in that part of the country. Assessments did the business for me there. There were a hundred and seventeen investments to one dividend, and the proportion of income to the outlay was a little against me...I am willing to sell all that property and throw in the improvements. Perhaps you remember that celebrated "North Ophir"? I bought that mine. It was very rich in pure silver. You could take it out in lumps as large as a filbert. But when it was discovered that those lumps were melted half dollars, and hardly melted at that, a painful cast of "salting" was apparent, and the undersigned adjourned to the poor-house again. I paid assessments on Hale and Norcross until they sold me out, and I had to take in washing for a living--and the next month that infamous stock went up to $7,000 a foot. I own millions and millions of feet of affluent silver leads in Nevada--in fact, I own the entire undercrust of that country nearly, and if Congress would move that state off my property so I could get at it, I would be wealthy yet...If you know of any one desiring a permanent investment, I can furnish him one that will have the virtue of being eternal.

Twain's claims are exaggerated but you get the picture.

Virginia City was still a young mining camp. The rough element strutted around town shooting and knifing each other and sometimes innocent bystanders. When a knife or gun fight broke out in one of the many saloons, a crowd of men rushed out the front doors. Murders and violence were so commonplace *Enterprise* reporters wrote off a murder with a single line or short paragraph.

For a time during the early days, the chief desperado was as respected as the banker, editor or chief gambler. The best known names in the Territory were long-tailed gunslingers, men who lived at the edge of death and traveled with their lives in their hands. These men generally killed amongst themselves and seldom troubled peacable citizens for killing a man who was without a notorious reputation was pointless. Twain wrote of this in *Roughing It*:

I remember an instance of a desperado's contempt for such small game as a private citizen's life. I was taking a late supper in a restaurant one night, with two reporters and a little printer named--Brown, for instance--any name will do. Presently a stranger with a long-tailed coat on came in, and not noticing Brown's hat, which was lying in a chair, sat down on it. Little Brown sprang up and became abusive in a moment. The stranger smiled, smoothed out the hat, and offered it to Brown with profuse apologies couched in caustic sarcasm, and begged Brown not to destroy him. Brown threw off his coat and challenged the man to a fight--abused him, threatened him, impeached his courage, and urged and even implored him to fight; and in the mean time the smiling stranger placed himself under our protection in mock distress. But presently he assumed a serious tone, and said:

"Very well, gentlemen, if we must fight, we must, I suppose. But don't rush into danger and then say I gave you no warning. I am more than a match for all of you when I get started, I will give you proofs, and then if my friend here still insists, I will try to accommodate him."

The table we were sitting at was about five feet long, and unusually cumbersome and heavy. He asked us to put our hands on the dishes and hold them in their places a moment--one of them was a large oval dish with a portly roast on it. Then he sat down, tilted up one end of the table, set two of the legs on his knees, took the end of the table between his teeth, took his hands away, and pulled down on his teeth till the table came up to a level position, dishes and all! He said he could lift a keg of nails with his teeth. He picked up a common glass tumbler and bit a semicircle out of it. Then he opened his bosom and showed us a network of knife and bullet scars; showed us more on his arms and face, and said he believed he had bullets enough in his body to make a pig of lead. He was armed to the teeth. He closed with a remark that he was Mr._____ of Cariboo--a celebrated name whereat we shook in our shoes. I would publish the name, but for the suspicion that he might come and carve me. He finally inquired if Brown still thirsted for blood. Brown turned the thing over in his mind a moment, and then--asked him to supper.

In May, Twain and Clement Rice, the Unreliable, left Virginia City for a month's stay in San Francisco. The trip was a four week party during which Twain fell in love with San Francisco. Twain and Rice attended balls and ate at the poshest restaurants. During this first trip to San Francisco, Twain met and became friends with local reporters and editors. He made a connection with the San Francisco *Call* for which he began writing occasional correspondent letters from Virginia City. Twain would later work for the *Call* after leaving Virginia City.

In, "Over The Mountains", published in the *Enterprise*, later in the *Golden Era*, Mark Twain tells of the stage ride across the Sierra Nevada mountains to Sacramento. This article reflects the rough, Western humor Twain would popularize in *Roughing It*. The famous stage driver in this piece may have been based on Hank. Twain advised readers to ride outside the stagecoach despite its dangers:

...An outside seat is preferable, though, day or night. All you want to do is to prepare for it thoroughly. You should sleep forty-eight hours in succession before starting so that you may not have to do anything of that kind on the box. You should also take a heavy overcoat with you. I did neither...I almost shivered the shirt off myself during that long night ride from Strawberry to Folsom. Our driver was a very companionable man, though, and this was a happy circumstance for me, because, being drowsy and worn out, I would have gone to sleep and fallen overboard if he had not enlivened the dreary hours with his conversation. Whenever I stopped coughing, and went to nodding, he always watched me out of the corner of his eye until I got to pitching in his direction, and then he would stir me up and inquire if I were asleep. If I said "No" (and I was apt to do that), he always said "it was a bully good thing for me that I warn't, you know", and then went on to relate cheerful anec-

dotes of people who had got to nodding by his side and when he wasn't noticing, they had fallen off and broken their necks. He said he could see those fellows before him now, all jammed and bloody and quivering in death's agony...

...I was awake...The driver took up the thread of his discourse and proceeded to soothe me again: "As I was saying, I see a poor cuss tumble off along here one night--he was monstrous drowsy, and went to sleep when I'd took my eye off of him for a moment-- and he fetched up agin a bouder, and in a second there wasn't anything left of him but a promiscus pile of hash! It was moonlight, and when I got down and looked at him he was quivering like jelly, and sorter moaning to himself, like, and the bones of his legs was sticking out through his pantaloons every which way, like that." (Here the driver mixed his fingers up after the manner of a stack of muskets, and illuminated them with the ghostly light of his cigar.) "He warn't in misery long though. In a minute and half he was deader 'n smelt--Bob!" In this way the genial driver caused the long hours to pass sleeplessly away...

About June 1, Twain and the Unreliable returned to Virginia City. June 3, the Virginia *Union* wrote that, "Mark Twain was at the Firemen's ball last night dressed in a most ridiculous manner. He had on a linen coat, calf-skin vest and a pair of white pants, the whole set off with a huge pair of buffalo shoes and lemon colored kids..."

Twain had written his mother about his high times in San Francisco. Jane Clemens, always concerned with her son's behavior, questioned him about the company he kept and where he got his money. July 18, Twain wrote his mother the following letter which gives insight into his day to day life:

My Dear Mother and Sister

Ma, you are slinging insinuations at me again. Such as "Where did I get the money?" and "The company I kept" in San Francisco." Why I sold "Wildcat" mining ground that was given me, and my credit was always good at the bank for two or three thousand dollars, and is yet. I never gamble, in any shape or manner, and never drink anything stronger than lager beer, which conduct is regarded as miraculously temperate in this country. As for my company, Ma, I went into the very best society to be found in San Francisco, and to do that, you must know, of course, that I had to keep myself mighty straight. I also move in the best Society of Virginia, and actually have a reputation to preserve.

As for money, I managed to make a living, but if I had any business tact, the office of reporter here would be worth $30,000 a year--where as, if I get 4 or $5,000 out of it, it will be as much as I expect. I have stock in my possession which, if I had sold when it was first given me, from time to time, in the last months, would have brought me $10,000--but I have carelessly let it go to nothing again. I don't think I am any account, anyhow. Now, I raised the price of "North Ophir" from $13 a foot to $45 a foot, today, and they gave me five feet. That will go the way of all the rest. I shall pro-bably mislay it or throw it in my trunk and never get a dollar out of it. But I am telling you too many secrets, and I'll stop. One more. A gentleman in San Francisco asked me to call at his office, and he would give me five feet of "Overman". Well, do you know I never went after it? The stock is worth $400.00 a foot, now--$2,000 thrown away. I don't care a straw, for myself, but I ought to have had more thought for you. Nevermind, though, Ma--I will be more cereful in future, I will take care that your expenses are paid--sure.

You and Pamela only pay $8 a week apiece for board (and lodg-ing too?) Well, you are not in an expensive part of the world, cer-tainly. My room-mate and I pay, together, $70 a month for our bed-chamber, and $50 a month, each, for board, besides. Put in my washing, and it costs me $100 a month to live.

Affectionately,
Mark

"Mark Twain" had become such a part of Clemens' life that he signed his name "Mark," in this letter to his own mother.

Twain was given five feet of "North Ophir" as reward for boosting the mine in his column, a common practice at that time which put extra income in Twain's pockets. Twain enclosed a twenty dollar bill in this letter to his mother. Sam and Orion faithfully supported their mother financially.

Toward the end of July, the *Enterprise* was moved to its new brick building; it was just in time, for a terrible fire burned half the town to the ground. The *Enterprise* building was unscathed but Mark Twain's boarding house, the White House, was burned down. Twain lost all of his clothing and a trunk full of mining stock. The next day a passing acquaintance gave him a handful of wildcat stock. Twain sold the stock and bought a new suit.

"On the day of the fire my constitution succumbed to a severe cold, caused by undue exertion in getting ready to do something," Twain wrote in "Curing A Cold." August 11, Twain accompanied by "Young Wilson, otherwise known as the Unimportant, left Virginia City for Lake Tahoe in an attempt to cure his cold. From there he took the stage to Steamboat Springs, located in Washoe Valley about 12 miles from Virginia City. He stayed at Steamboat Springs resort for several days, trying to cure the same cold. There, Twain wrote several articles for the *Enterprise*; one, "Curing A Cold," was later published in the *Golden Era*. In an article written for the *Enterprise*, Twain tells of a strange concoction he was given called a "Wake-up Jake," in an attempt to cure his cold.

> ...*The Doctor hesitated a moment, and then fixed up as repulsive a mixture as ever was stirred together in a table-spoon. I swallowed the nauseous mess, and that one meal sufficed me for the space of forty-eight hours. And during all that time, I could not have enjoyed a viler taste in my mouth if I had swallowed a slaughter-house. I lay down with all my clothes on, and with an utter indifference to my fate here or hereafter, and slept like a statue from six o'clock until noon. I got up, then, the sickest man that ever yearned to vomit and couldn't. All the dead and decaying matter in nature seemed buried in my stomach, and I "heaved, and retched, and heaved again," but I could not compass a resurrection--my dead would not come forth. Finally, after rumbling, and growling and producing agony and chaos within me for many hours, the dreadful dose began its work, and for the space of twelve hours it vomited me, and purged me, and likewise caused me to bleed at the nose.*
> *I came out of that siege as weak as an infant...*

Twain was back in Virginia City, August 24; his cold was still with him. In another attempt to cure his cold, Twain left for San Francisco September 5th. The Virginia *Evening Bulletin* reported that day that,

> *...Mark had made his mark in a remarkable manner upon the good will of the people of Virginia, among whom he has hosts of warm friends. It is said that Mark contemplates making the fearful leap from bachelorhood to matrimony. We don't believe it--but true or not, he has our best wishes for his welfare, whether running single or in twain.*

The *Gold Hill News* also reported that Twain had asked a young lady to marry him. Who the woman was is unknown. Apparently, she did not accept his invitation.

Arriving in San Francisco, Twain was advised as to how to cure his cold. Twain wrote, "a lady at the hotel told me to drink a quart of whisky every twenty-four hours, and a friend up town recommended precisely the same course. Each advised me to take a quart; that made a half a gallon. I did it, and still live."

In mid-October, Twain returned from San Francisco. Dan De Quille was back from his long absence and was again reporting for the *Enterprise*. Twain and Dan decided to share an apartment at 25 North B Street.

Dan De Quille and Mark Twain were as unlike as two men could be, yet they got along well with one another. Mark Twain said that he and De Quille never had an argument during the time they lived and reported together. This is saying a lot for De Quille. Twain was easily unnerved and he liked having his own way; he demanded a lot from friends.

De Quille was six years older than Twain; he was tall and slender and wore a beard. De Quille was shy, gentle, dependable and had an even temperament. He was a diligent writer and strove for accuracy. De Quille believed his most important job was to accurately report mining news. He daily inspected the mines and new strikes. Unlike Mark Twain, he enjoyed dealing with facts and numbers. De Quille had a whimsical, gentle sense of humor and was considered Virginia City's best humorist and was well respected throughout the Pacific Coast.

Twain, on the other hand, was brash, impulsive erratic. He had no patience for facts and figures and preferred writing about events which he could interpret in his own individual style. He was not dependable and he was always late. Twain made readers laugh but he also insulted some. Making fun of local characters sometimes got him into trouble. One angered citizen stormed into the *Enterprise* offices and threatened to boot Mark Twain all over the Territory. "Well," Twain said to the man, "if you've got money enough to put me all over these toll-roads just start in." That was typical Twain. Twain got the reader's attention by exaggeration; his humor was not gentle nor inoffensive.

Though Twain and De Quille were equal in talent, Twain's desire for notoriety would help him to achieve national success. De Quille would remain a mining camp reporter his entire life which is all he cared to be.

De Quille later wrote of his associations with Mark Twain:

...We were both young then, and the world seemed young and teeming to overflowing with wealth. The whole country was booming, and the Enterprise *was booming equally with all else. It was undoubtedly at the time the most flourishing newspaper on the Pacific Coast. A tidal wave of gold rolled in upon its proprietors. The paper seemed to run itself--and in doing so ran all connected with it. It seemed to take the lead and go right along without thought or care on the part of anyone. All there was to do was to pile into the paper all the news it would hold. The money to pay for everything seemed to besiege the office.*

Mark Twain and I were employed in the local department of the Enterprise, *and there was no lack of matters of interest in our line. Improvements of all kinds, new discoveries in the mines, accidents, cutting and shooting affrays, fires and all manner of exciting events crowded themselves upon us. However, we went merrily along, joking and laughing, and never feeling the weight of the work we were doing in the whirl and excitement of the times.*

Soon after we began working together Mark and I rented two rooms on the second floor of a large brick building on B Street erected by R. M. Daggett and his partner W.F. Meyers, the well known operator in mining stocks. We had a large bedroom and a somewhat smaller room for use as a parlor sitting room...We had a huge double bed, piles of bedding, splendid carpets and fine fittings of all kinds. This, in comparison with the bunks in which we roosted in an old tumble-down shed when I first began work on the

Enterprise, was quite palatial...

Joseph T. Goodman...bossed the job of furnishing these rooms, and piled into them several hundred dollars worth of stuff. Mark said that as Goodman had been "so keen to do the ordering" of the things, we'd "just let him foot the bill". So, whenever the furniture man--good old Moses Goldman--came after us with his bill, we laughed at him, and referred him to Goodman. But one day old Moses sued us and we had to square up with him. Mark said we might have known better than to try such a trick with "a man whose front name was Moses and whose rear name was Goldman."

Mark and I agreed well as room-mates. Both wanted to read and smoke about the same length of time after getting into bed, and if one got hungry and got up to go down town for oysters the other also bacame hungry and turned out.

We had in the building where we roomed a very agreeable and jolly lot of people. Tom Fitch, the "Silver Tongued," his wife, sister-in-law and mother-in-law occupied a large suite of rooms just across the hall from us and were the best neighbors. Often when Mark and I got home at night we found laid out for us in our rooms a fine spread of pie, cake, milk and the like. Mrs. Fitch's mince pies were perfection.

Envious reporters of other papers did not scruple to assert that we stole all these good things out of the Fitch pantry. We denied the charge, but it was labor lost. Worse than this was their story of our having hanged the pet cat of Tom's mother-in-law. It was said that we tied a cord about the neck of the cat and suspended it from a rear second-story window. As the good old lady had actually lost her cat, she was a little sour with us for a few days. It afterward appeared that R. M. Daggett, who was a great friend of the Fitch family, knew of the old lady's loss, and put reporters of the other papers up to publishing a sensational story on the "Secret Midnight Hanging". The explanation in the last line or two that the victim was a cat, made it all the worse for us with the old lady. For about a fortnight mince pies did not flow upon us.

A good deal has been said first and last of the stealing of Tom Fitch's firewood while Mark and I were rooming at the Dagget and Meyers building. Tom never lost much wood through us, but the boys would always have it otherwise. Wood was something of an object in those days, as in winter it sometimes boomed up to $40 a cord. We were in the habit of buying of the Chinese wood-peddlers by the donkey load. One bitterly cold night we found ourselves without wood. In the hall on the same floor stood Tom's well filled wood box. Said Mark: "We are not going to freeze in here with plenty of wood just outside our door," and out he went and gathered up an armful of Tom's wood. Coming back to our door with a bang, he faced about in it as if he had just come from the inside and sang out in an angry tone, as though to me in the hall: "Dan, damn it all, don't be taking Tom's wood! It ain't right, and wood so confounded high! It ain't a nice thing to do. Now take that wood right back or there'll be trouble!"

He then went back to the wood box and made a big racket, but when he threw down one stick he picked up two, and presently he came into the room with wood piled up to his chin. This he put down so carefully that the sticks wouldn't have broken an egg. We soon had a rousing fire and wood to spare for the morning.

There was plenty of such fun in those times. A trick of outsiders was to place all manner of things in our rooms, the doors of which were never locked. Mark had a Japanese sword. One night when we got home we were startled to find standing before us a gigantic fellow who seemed in the dim light of an open window to threaten us with a drawn sword. Of course it was expected we would turn loose upon the giant sword with our pistols. Luckily, however, we hailed the intruder, offering him a chance for his life, and by doing so discovered the hoax...

San Francisco Examiner, March 19, 1893

...Mark and I agreed well in our work, which we divided when there was a rush of events, but we often cruised in company--he taking the items of news he could best handle, and I such as I felt myself competent to work up. However, we wrote at the same table and frequently helped each other with such suggestions as occurred to us during the brief consulatations we held, in regard to the handling of any matters of importance. Never was there an angry word between us in all the time we worked together.

Mark Twain, as a reporter, was earnest and enthusiastic in such work as suited him--really industrious--but when it came to "cast-iron" items, he gave them "a lick and a promise." He hated to have to do with figures and measurements and solid facts, such as were called for in matter pertaining to mines and machinery.

Mark displayed a peculiarity when at work that was very detrimental to the integrity of office property. In case he wished to clip an item, or paragraph out of a paper, and could not at once lay his hand upon his scissors, he would cut out the required matter with his knife, at the same time slashing into the baize covering of the table. His end of the cover was so mutilated that little was left on the original cloth...

Mark Twain was pretty apt in sketching in a rude way, and when reporting meetings where there were long waits, or uninteresting debates, he would cover the margins of his copy paper with drawings. When reporting the meetings of the Board of Aldermen, where there was often much tedious talk, he would frequently make sketches illustrative of the subjects under discussion. Some of his off-hand sketches were very good--good in the same way that a pun is sometimes good, though farfetched and ridiculous...I recall one...that might have been labeled "The Captured Menagerie." There had been some trouble about collecting city licenses from a menagerie...and the matter came up before the Board of Aldermen. Mark was amused at the talk of what could be done and what would be done with the show and the showmen if the license was not paid at once and so he pictured it all out. He depicted the City Marshal leading away the elephant by its trunk, and the Mayor mounted upon a giraffe which he had captured, while one policeman had a lion by the tail, and another had captured a rhinocerous. Others still had shouldered kangaroos, strings of monkeys and the like...

California Illustrated Magazine, August, 1893

CHAPTER TEN

The Massacre At Dutch Nick's

Mark Twain published his most well know story for the *Enterprise* October 28, 1863. It was an awful tale of murder and violence. The story first stunned readers; then it made them angry. It has since been called the "Massacre at Dutch Nick's" and this story, more than any other piece of Twain's *Enterprise* writing, made Mark Twain known to Western readers.

Mark Twain told unsuspecting readers,

> *...P. Hopkins or Phillip Hopkins, has been residing with his family in the old log house just at the edge of the great pine forest which lies between Empire City and Dutch Nick's. The family consisted of 9 children--5 girls and 4 boys--the oldest of the group, Mary, being 19 years old, and the youngest, Tommy, about a year and a half...*
>
> *...About 10 o'clock on Monday evening Hopkins dashed into Carson on horseback, with his throat cut from ear to ear, and bearing in his hand a reeking scalp from which the warm, smoking blood was still dripping, and fell in a dying condition in front of the Magnolia Saloon. Hopkins expired in the course of five minutes, without speaking. The long red hair of the scalp he bore marked it as that of Mrs. Hopkins. A number of citizens, headed by Sheriff Gasherie, mounted at once and rode down to Hopkin's house, where a ghastly scene met their gaze. The scalpless corpse of Mrs. Hopkins lay across the threshhold, with her head split open and her right hand almost severed from the wrist. Near her lay the ax*

with which the murderous deed had been committed. In one of the bedrooms six of the children were found, one in bed and the others scattered about the floor. They were all dead. Their brains had evidently been dashed out with a club, and every mark about them seemed to have been made with a blunt instrument. The children must have struggled hard for their lives, as articles of their clothing and broken furniture were strewn about the room in the utmost confusion. Julia and Emma, aged ...14 and 17, were found in the kitchen, bruised and insensible, but it is thought recovery is possible...

...Hopkins...had been a heavy owner in the best mines of Virginia and Gold Hill, but when the San Francisco papers exposed the game of cooking dividends in order to bolster up our stocks he grew afraid and sold out, and invested to an immense amount in the Spring Valley Water Company of San Francisco. He was advised to do this by a relative of his, one of the editors of the San Francisco Bulletin...

Shortly after Hopkins had invested all his capital in the Spring Valley Water Company,

several dividends were cooked on this...property...Spring Valley stock went down to nothing...It is presumed that this misfortune drove him mad and resulted in his killing himself and the greater portion of his family.

Newspapers up and down the Pacific Coast immediately reprinted the story believing it was true. The next day Mark Twain published a single line, "I take it all back.--Twain."

Immediately, editors and readers throughout the West attacked Mark Twain and the *Enterprise* for publishing the gruesome hoax. The Reese River *Reveille* wrote, "Some of the papers are expressing astonishment that 'Mark Twain'...should perpetrate such a 'sell' as 'A Blody Massacre Near Carson'...They don't know him. We would not be surprised at ANYTHING done by that silly idiot." Another wrote. "The ass who originated the story doubtless thinks he is 'old smarty'--we don't." The Virginia *Evening Bulletin* said of the "Massacre,"

...Now in the item referred to, their is not a particle of truth, but unfortunately people at a distance may not be able to detect the self contradictions that are all through this extraordinary item, and will probably consider this wholesale murder as an "o'er true tale." God knows our Territory has a reputation of being the theatre of scenes of blood and violence that really do occur bad enough to satisfy our bitterest enemies. There does not exist any need to paint our characters any blacker than they really are. Those who have ever been in the Territory will well know that Dutch Nick's and Empire City are one and the same place, nor is there any log cabin, nor any family of nine children of the name of Hopkins living there, or ever did live there. The whole story is as baseless as the fabric of a dream.

October 28, 1863

Mark Twain had not intended to mislead the public. He meant the "Massacre" to be taken as a satire but he had written about the murders to convincingly and graphically. He intended the story to do several things: reveal the devious practice of falsely inflating stock prices, embarass San Francisco papers who should have warned the public of such schemes and to embarass Pete Hopkins, of the Magnolia Saloon who had offended Twain in some way.

Mark Twain placed his real message at the end of the article. But readers either did not read this portion or missed the point. Twain wrote:

...The newspapers of San Francisco permitted this water company to go on borrowing money and cooking dividends, under cover of which cunning financiers crept out of the tottering concern, leaving the crash to come upon poor and unsuspecting stockholders, without offering to expose the villainy at work. We hope the fearful massacre detailed above may prove the saddest result of their silence.

Twain was shocked when local readers took the story seriously. He believed the details of the murder made it obvious that it was all a satire. Nor did he consider that other newspapers outside the area would publish the story. In, "My Bloody Massacre," he wrote:

...The murderer was perfectly well known to every creature in the land as a bachelor, and consequently he could not murder his wife and nine children; ...there was not a "great pine forest between Empire City and Dutch Nick's," there wasn't a solitary tree within fifteen miles of either place; and, finally, it was ...notorious that Empire City and Dutch Nick's were one and the same place...on top of all these absurdities I stated that this...murderer, after inflicting a wound upon himself that the reader ought to have seen would kill an elephant in the twinkling of an eye, jumped on his horse and rode four miles, waving his wife's reeking scalp in the air...

Dutch Nick's, or Empire City as it was later known, is a desert spot 4 miles east of Carson City on the Carson River right off Highway 50. Today an industrial area surrounds the old Empire City graveyard where "Dutch Nick," Nick Ambrose is buried. It is dusty and full of sagebrush. The place has never known the shadow of a tree never mind a whole forest. During the 1870's many large mining mills were located on the Carson River in or near Empire City.

The grave of Nicholaus Ambrose, "Dutch Nick," in the Empire City Cemetery. *Larry Tanner photo.*

Mark Twain did not appreciate the wrath heaped upon him by other papers. He angrily responded to their attacks. Twain called the writer of the *Bulletin's* attack, a "little person, oyster-brained idiot." But his defense could not hold back the wave of outrage. The *Bulletin* came back with:

POOR WRETCH, WE PITY HIM.--That unhappy mortal, the local of the Enterprise, appears to be in a terrible agony at the castigation which he is receiving for the sin he committed in publishing that rascally hoax. Out of pity for the poor wretch's misery, we will not retort upon him, and as a mark of the profundity of our pity for his sufferings, we advise him to depart in peace and sin no more. If he will drop that sin of well, we won't name it--"That doth so easily beset him," and leave off going to Chinatown, stop drinking whisky, pay his washerwoman, get up early, and not make a night hideous by howling his sorrows to the winds, he may yet become a partially decent member of society...

Mark Twain, well aware of his own shortcomings, did not take these attacks well. They made him angry and eventually they depressed him. He meant the story to do good but readers had missed his point. Dan De Quille wrote:

...All this worried Mark as I had never before seen him worried. Said he: "I am being burned alive on both sides of the mountains." ...One night when the persecution was hottest, he was so distressed he could not sleep. He tossed, tumbled and groaned aloud. So I set to work to comfort him. "Mark," said I, "never mind this bit of a gale, it will soon blow itself out. This item of yours will be remembered and talked about when all your other work is forgotten. The murder at Dutch Nick's will be quoted for years from now as the big sell of these times."

Said Mark: "I believe you are right; I remember I once did a thing at home in Missouri, was caught at it and worried almost to death. I was a mere lad and was going to school in a little town where I had an uncle living. I at once left the town and did not return to it for three years. When I finally came back I found I was only remembered as 'the boy that played the trick on the school master."

Reporting with Mark Twain

According to De Quille,

> ...Mark's whole object in writing the story was to make the murderer go to Pete Hopkin's saloon and fall dead in front of it-- Pete having in some way offended him. I could never quite see how this was to hurt Pete Hopkins. Mark probably meant to insinuate that the murderer had been rendered insane by the kind of liquor sold over the Hopkin's bar, or that he was one of Pete's bosom friends...
>
> *Reporting with Mark Twain*

Pete Hopkins ran the Magnolia Saloon in Carson City. Twain may have wanted to get back at Hopkins and used the "Massacre" to do so. That was like him. Years later, he said of his intentions:

> ...Once more, in my self-complacent simplicity I felt that the time had arrived for me to rise up and be a reformer. I put this reformatory satire in the shape of a fearful "Massacre at Empire City." The San Francisco papers were making a great outcry about the inequity to the Daney Silver-Mining Company, whose directors had declared a "cooked" or false dividend, for the purposes of increasing the value of their stock, so that they could sell out at a comfortable figure, and then scramble from under the tumbling concern. And while abusing the Daney, those papers did not forget to urge the public to get rid of all their silver stocks and invest in sound and safe San Francisco stocks, such as the Spring Valley Water Company, etc. But right after this unfortunate juncture, behold the Spring Valley cooked a dividend too! And, so under the insidious mask of an invented "bloody massacre," I stole upon the public unawares with my scathing satire upon the dividend cooking system...
>
> *"My Bloody Massacre," Sketches New and Old*

Editors and readers clamored for Mark Twain's head. They wanted him fired from the *Enterprise* staff. Many subscribers cut off their subscriptions. Editors threatened never to rely on the *Enterprise* as long as Mark Twain wrote for the paper.

Twain, deeply hurt by the outrage offered to quit the paper. "Oh, Joe," he said, "I have ruined your business, and the only reparation I can make is to resign. You can never recover from this blow while I am on the paper."

"Nonsense," Goodman countered. "We can furnish the people with news, but we can't supply them with sense...The flurry will pass, you must go ahead. We'll win out in the long run." And they did.

For as long as Mark Twain remained with the *Enterprise*, he was kidded about having murdered the entire Hopkins family. It was a running joke and he tired of hearing it. But the "Massacre at Dutch Nick's" gave him notoriety and helped establish his reputation on the West Coast.

Years afterward, Dan De Quille wrote:

> *...Today not one man in a hundred in Nevada can remember anything written by Mark Twain while he was connected with the* Enterperise, *except this one item in regard to the shocking murder at Dutch Nick's; all else is forgotten, even by his oldest and most intimate friends.*

Mark Twain's "Massacre at Dutch Nick's," may have failed at its intended purposes. But the furor over the "Massacre," dramatically taught Twain the power of the written word to excite and move people. Writing well was a useful tool. Mark Twain was slowly realizing he possessed a powerful gift and writing was one of the ways he could communicate this gift to others.

CHAPTER ELEVEN

Artemus Ward Points The Way

One of the most important men Mark Twain met during his stay in Virginia City arrived just before Christmas, 1863. His real name was Charles F. Browne but he was known throughout America and Britain as Artemus Ward, a highly popular humorous writer and speaker. At twenty-eight, Ward was at the peak of his career. He had authored humorous books and articles; his articles and quips appeared regularly in newspapers and national magazines. He frequently lectured throughout America and Britian. Lecture isn't the right word; Ward's *show* was a stand-up comedy routine known as the "Babes in the Wood." Ward never mentioned the babes in the wood. He rambled for an hour or so about a wide range of topics. Ward's humor was based on ridiculous misspellings, mispronounciations, fumbled grammar, misuse of words, garbled and incoherent sentences. Ward was brilliant but he acted like an uneducated idiot, making hilarious comments dead-pan, pretending in embarassment not to understand why audiences roared. Ward was the common man's humorist, a sort of 1860's version of Rodney Dangerfield. Audiences loved him for his wit, warmth and humanity and Ward loved them back passionately.

Beneath Ward's seeming naivete and folksy manner was a young man who cared and had important things to say. There was social criticism, satire of human weakness, pretentiousness and sentimentality. Ward was clever in the way Mark Twain was clever. When Thomas Maguire wired him and asked, "What will you take for forty nights in California?" Ward answered, "Brandy and water."

Ward's coming to the Comstock was like Marilyn Monroe visiting the troops. Excitement shot through the mining towns like electricity. Ward was a great celebrity and the hard-pressed miners were hungry for outside entertainment.

Ward was scheduled to speak twice in Virginia City at Maguire's Opera House and once in Gold Hill and Silver City.

Artemus Ward's visit had a powerful impact on Mark Twain. When Mark Twain watched Ward's shows the lights went on; suddenly Twain realized how he might better use his humor both to entertain and make money: it was on the stage like Ward. After all, he made people laugh; he could entertain; he could do what Ward did and he would try. With Ward's appearance, Mark Twain's ideas for his future and his aspirations came together in a plan that would change his life.

Mark Twain was familiar with Ward's work. He announced Ward's coming to Virginia City in an article which imitated Ward's humorous writing:

> ...We understand that Artemus Ward contemplates visiting the region to deliver his lectures, and perhaps make some additions to his big "sho". In his last letter to us he appeared particularly anxious to "sekure a kupple ov horned todes; alsowe, a lizard which it may be persessed of 2 tales, or any komical snaix, an enny sich little unconsidered trifles, as the poets say, which they do not interest the kommun mind...Could you alsowe manage to govvel up the skulp of the layte Missus Hopkins? I adore sich foot-prints of atrocity as it were, muchly. I was roominatin on gitting a bust of mark Twain, but I've kwit kontemplatin the work. They tell me down heer to the Ba the the busts air so kommon it wood ony bee an waist of wax to git un kounterfit presentiment." We shall assist Mr. Ward in every possible way about making his Washoe collection and have no doubt but he will pick up many curious things during his sojourn.
> Golden Era, November 29, 1863

Artemus Ward arrived in Virginia City around December 23rd with his manager, E.E. Hingston. Mark Twain, Dan De Quille and Joe Goodman took Ward in like a brother. Ward made the *Enterprise* offices his home base and at times helped the boys get the paper out so they could get back to playing. Ward was only in Virginia City for a week but it was long enough for the four men to become friends for they were all Bohemians at heart. Mark Twain and Dan De Quille showed Ward the town. For an entire week, the boys went on a rampage; they raised hell, got drunk, carried on until dawn. In between parties, Ward gave his lectures. Years later, Dan De Quille recalled Ward's visit:

Virginia City was booming when Artemus Ward arrived to deliver his lecture. Comstockers received Artemus as a brother, and he seemed as much at home as if he had all his life been a resident of Virginia City. He remained on the Comstock several days, making the Enterprise his headquarters. Mark Twain and I had the pleasure of showing him the town, and a real pleasure it was--a sort of circus, in fact--as he constantly overflowed with fun. He was anxious to get hold of the lingo and style of the miners, and we made him acquainted with several old forty-niners. The greeting among these men struck him as something new, and he began practicing, playing himself off as an old-timer...

Artemus Ward was full of curiousity about the Piute Indians and the Chinese. While he was here the Chinese had a pow-wow of some kind. A big tent was erected on a vacant lot in Chinatown, in which half a dozen yellow and purple-robed priests from San Francisco displayed their gods and received the vows of the faithful. One night Mark, Ward and I "took in" this show and other Chinatown sights. We went to see Hop Sing, head of one company. Both insisted upon our testing various fiery drinks, such as rice "blandy" and other kinds of "blandy".

We narrowly escaped being caught in the midst of a fight that started between the rival companies, a fight in which about fifty shots were fired, killing one man and wounding two or three.

In returning to the city from Chinatown we concluded to take a "near cut". Coming to a string of low frame houses, Artemus said the nearest cut was over the tops of the shanties, and crying "Follow your leader!" mounted a shed and the roof of a house. "Come ahead," cried he, "and we'll go up into town over the roofs of the houses. Follow your leader."

The "China blandy" was venturesome...soon we were all marching along over the roofs. We had not proceeded far before there came to our ears the command, "Halt there or I shoot," and we saw a man with a shotgun leveled at us. The man who had halted us was a watchman. He held his gun on us until we climbed down and marched up to him as ordered. Explanations followed and all was right as soon as our names were given.

"Right your are," said Artemus. "Take a few tickets and come to my show," and he poked over the fence to the man a handful of tickets.

"Thanks," said the watchman, and reaching behind into the tail of a long coat he drew forth a bottle that was almost as long as the barrel of his gun. "Good stuff," said he, as he poked the long bottle over the fence to us.

Mark and I feared to mix fighting American whisky with warlike Chinese "blandy", but Artemus took the bottle, and as he placed it to his lips and elevated it toward the North Star it looked like a telescope. "Splendid," said he, as he lowered the "instrument."

After this adventure we concluded to go to our rooms on B Street and all three turn into our big bed together, "three saints," as Artemus put it, "Mark, Luke and John." However, in going up Sutton Avenue there was heard "a sound of revelry by night." We were passing a huge barn of a building in which a couple of hurdy-gurdies were holding forth. Hurdies were something new to Ward, and he said he wanted to see this show.

On entering the dance hall Artemus announced our arrival by stating that we were "Babes in the Wood." As he was known by sight to most of those present there were at once "Cheers for Artemus Ward."

"Now," said Ward, "we three have got to have a dance together. It'll be a thing our offspring to the furthest generation will be proud of!"

So selecting three stalwart and capable girls as partners we danced to the unbounded admiration of a large and enthusiastic audience headed by "Kettle-belly" Brown.

Artemus threw a twenty-dollar gold piece on the bar to pay for the dances and beer. The bartender took out about four times the usual rates and was raking Ward's double eagle into the till when "Kettle's" big hand came down upon the gold with a startling spat.

"No you don't!" said "Kettle", "these gentlemen are friends of mine. This twenty don't go into the till until you hand out the right change!" Instantly the correct change was passed over to Ward.

Immediately the whole heart and soul of Artemus Ward went out to "Kettle." Said he to Brown: "We are three mere 'Babes in the Wood'; come along with us. We need you to take care of us."

So instead of going to bed we went forth under the guidance of the genial "Kettle". We went to hear the Cornish singers, and to see some of the big games, meeting with still further adventures in our wanderings, but everywhere fathered and guarded by the bulky, whole-souled and honest old Sonora miner, "Kettle-belly" Brown.

The first rays of the morning sun were guilding the peak of Mount Davidson. The "Babes" were out in front of Aaron Hooper's saloon--where happened to be some convenient packing cases--for a mouthful of fresh air...

San Francisco *Examiner*, March 19, 1893

James "Kettle Belly" Brown, miner, sport and fire chief with whom Mark Twain, Artemus Ward and Dan De Quille spent one famous evening painting the town.

Mark Twain, Dan De Quille and Joe Goodman attended each of Ward's performances. Mark Twain admired Ward's humor and respected his success. Twain studied Ward's performance, noted the techniques Ward used to work his audience. Twain would later employ some of Ward's techniques in his own performances. Twain was impressed by Ward's "Babes in the Wood" and wrote,

> *There are perhaps fifty subjects treated in it, and there is a passable point in every one of them, and a healthy laugh, also, for any of God's creatures...The man who is capable of listening to the 'Babes in the Wood' from beginning to end without laughing either inwardly or outwardly must have done murder, or least meditated it, at some time in during his life.*
>   Virginia Evening *Bulletin, December 28, 1863*

During his visit, Ward and Twain spoke of their careers. Ward realized Twain was an emerging talent. He encouraged Mark to

The "Three Saints," as Artemus Ward put it. Left to right, Artemus Ward, Dan De Quille and Mark Twain. *Nevada Historical Society.*

seek an Eastern audience for his writings and offered to write on Twain's behalf a "powerfully convincing note" of introduction to the editor of the New York *Mercury*. Less than two months later, Mark Twain's first Eastern article, "For Sale or to Rent", was published in the *Mercury*, February 7, 1864, followed two weeks later by "Those Blasted Children." The publication of these articles was likely due to Ward's intervention on Mark Twain's behalf. These articles and the publication of "The Jumping Frog of Calaveras County" in the New York *Saturday Press* in 1865, helped establish Mark Twain's reputation in the East.

The meeting of Artemus Ward was a definite turning point in Mark Twain's writing career. Ward had inspired Mark Twain and instilled in his mind a new vision of his future. Almost immediately after Ward's visit, Twain's writing improved dramatically. Mark Twain very obviously took his writing more seriously. Twain was no longer merely filling columns. He really had something to say which he believed was important. His articles were now more direct, frank and often critical of political stupidity and human greed. Readers noticed the change in Twain's approach and the change gradually won their respect. Mark Twain had played the fool with his pranks but now the fool had suddenly become a shrewd, perceptive, caring writer whose moments of brilliance startled backyard readers.

Ward's visit reawakened Twain's desire to perform on the stage. He had toyed with the idea of becoming an actor but had not pursued it. Twain loved talking, he was good at it and enjoyed having people's undivided attention. After watching Ward perform, Mark Twain realized this was something he could do well and make money at.

Less than a month later, Mark Twain gave his first lecture at Carson City, a benefit for the First Presbyterian Church for which Orion was an elder. Mark Twain's lecture attracted a larger audience than Ward. The room was packed; at a dollar a head, Twain raised more than $200 for the church. Twain's first lecture was a great success and the beginning of a highly successful speaking career which lasted the rest of his life.

In Artemus Ward, Mark Twain saw his future as a nationally known writer and platform lecturer. Through Ward's encouragement and inspiration, Mark Twain stepped closer to that goal.

CHAPTER TWELVE

Mark Twain Matures

Mark Twain entered an important transition period in November, 1863 which lasted until the end of February, 1864. During these four months, Mark Twain was transformed from a prankster journalist to a serious, committed writer. His writing improved in content and style. His reputation as a humorist and journalist grew; he won the respect of peers and readers. His writing made a genuine impact on the Nevada community. Most importantly, Mark Twain realized he was a writer and his work could affect the world.

Mark Twain spent the greatest portion of this transition in Carson City as a political reporter for the *Enterprise*. November 2, he arrived in Carson City to report the Constitutional Convention. He made a brief trip to Virginia City in early December but was back in Carson for the close of the Convention, December 11. Exhausted from the whirl of day and night politics, December 12, he left for Lake Tahoe by himself for a rest. Twain was back in Virginia City for Artemus Ward's arrival December 23. He returned to Carson City shortly after New Year's, 1864. January 12 to February 20, he reported the third Territorial Legislature.

During this four month transition period, a number of positive influences came to bear on Mark Twain. These influences helped Mark Twain improve his writing and realize his potential as an important writer.

Fellow *Enterprise* journalists had definitely influenced Mark Twain's writing development during the thirteen months he had reported for the *Enterprise*.

Joe Goodman had taught Twain to adhere to facts in his reporting and Twain had largely followed Goodman's advice. There were the occasional bursts of fiction, the "Petrified Man," and the "Massacre At Dutch Nick's" but these had only increased his reputation as a humorist and regional celebrity. Rollin Daggett had taught Twain to speak his mind and attack wrong doing and injustice at any level. Jim Townsend, a marvelous story teller whose humor and style was much like Mark Twain's, had shared many stories with Mark Twain during long bull sessions. These stories and Townsend's style would work their way into Mark's writing. Dan De Quille, who had recently returned to Virginia City and with whom Twain was then living, was a positive example of a hard working journalist who took his work seriously and strove for accuracy. Dan encouraged Mark and often made helpful suggestions which tempered Twain's radical writing. Most importantly, within the *Enterprise* family Mark Twain found acceptance as a person and as a writer. The *Enterprise* staff was a constant source of friendship, inspiration and support.

Another important factor helping Mark Twain grow as a writer, was his increased writing output during this period. Five days a week, he wrote a 4,000 word political dispatch. On Sunday, he wrote a long personalized summary of political and social doings. Mark Twain was daily pumping out the equivalent of ten, typed, double-spaced pages, six days a week, sixty pages a week! In one month, Mark Twain wrote enough to fill two books. Those who considered Twain lazy, may not have realized the energy and time good writing requires. Writing is hard work, even for a writer as talented as Mark Twain. More than just pushing a pencil, writing well requires hours of intense concentration and thought. Anyone who has struggled with a twenty page term paper knows this. To add to the difficulties, the invention of the typewriter was years away. Everything had to be hand written in pencil or with ink and quill. If a writer made a mistake or wished to change a sentence, he either crossed it out and made a mess or rewrote the entire article by hand. To say the least, it was a grind which required time, labor and committment.

Another important factor was Mark Twain's change in attitude toward his work. Where in the past he collected or invented news simply to fill his columns, now Mark Twain had something to say which he believed was important. He was taking his writing more seriously. As political reporter for the most powerful newspaper in the Territory, Twain understood his responsibilities as a journalist. His articles were now largely concerned with issues which affected the community and the Territory. Twain was concerned about the burgeoning state. His humor and satire were still there, but his articles were far more frank. He possessed a new confidence and belief in his ideas and he worked hard in his columns to win people to his thinking.

This change in attitude may have partially been caused by Mark Twain's growing older. November 30, he turned twenty-eight. Practical minded, Mark Twain appears to have finally committed himself to writing as his career. His heightened regional success, Artemus Ward's visit, encouragement and inspiration had certainly helped him make up his mind.

Other important influences on his writing and thinking during this period were the intelligent, educated and agressive men with whom Twain daily and often nightly interacted. Most were attorneys, skilled with words in writing and speaking. Living and working among the best men in Nevada Territory for the greater part of four months no doubt stimulated Mark Twain.

Among these men was Alexander "Sandy" Baldwin. At twenty-two, Baldwin was one of the leading attorneys in Nevada Territory. Baldwin was brilliant; at fourteen he entered the University of Virginia; at ninteen he was a district attorney in California. As an attorney, Baldwin quickly earned over a half million dollars representing mining companies in litigation. Bill Stewart was often one of Baldwin's adversaries. During one courtroom battle, Baldwin kept interupting Stewart until Stewart shouted at Baldwin, "You little shrimp, if you interrupt me again, I'll eat you."

"If you do, you'll have more brains in your belly than you've ever had in your head." Baldwin was afterward U.S. District Court Judge in Nevada Territory.

It was Sandy Baldwin along with Theodore Winters who gave Mark Twain a $200 watch as a gift for his election as the President of the Third House, a group of reporters, legislators and citizens who gathered in saloons to ridicule legislative proceedings.

William "Bill" Stewart was the most prominent lawyer in

Nevada. He was tall, intelligent, witty and a brilliant courtroom strategist. Stewart made a fortune representing Virginia City mining companies and owned the finest house in Carson City.

Born in New York, raised in Ohio, Stewart attended Yale before coming to Caifornia in 1850. He became a prospector, studied law and was admitted to the California bar in 1852. In 1854 he was Attorney General of California. In 1860, Stewart came to Nevada, served as a member of the Territorial Council in 1861 and the Constitutional Convention of 1863 where Stewart lobbied against the taxation of mining properties.

Bill Stewart and James Nye were the first Nevadans elected to the Senate in 1864. Stewart served two long terms: 1864-75 and 1887-1905.

Three years after Mark Twain left Virginia City, he showed up at Bill Stewart's home in Washington, D.C. Twain told Stewart he was writing a book, *The Innocents Abroad*, and needed a temporary job. Bill Stewart hired Twain as his personal secretary and allowed him to live at his home in Washington, D.C.

William "Billy" Claggett was a boyhood friend of Sam Clemens'. Clemens met Claggett in Keokuk, Iowa while working for Orion's newspaper. Claggett was then studying law.

Clemens and Claggett were reunited in Carson City in the winter of 1861-62. Claggett traveled with Clemens to Unionville that winter on a wild goose chase for mountains of silver. Their hilarious journey is told in *Roughing It*. Claggett remained at Unionville where he practiced law. There he was elected to the Legislature in 1862 and to the House of Representatives in 1864. Claggett was known for his great oratorical skill and his mop of unruly hair.

Jack Simmons was Speaker of the House during the second Territorial Legislature. He was a close friend of Mark Twain's and a leading member of the Third House.

Abraham Curry was the principal founder of Carson City. Curry came to Nevada Territory in 1858 and prospected in Gold Canyon. He was one of the discoverers of the Gould and Curry mine, one of the richest Virginia City mines. Curry sold his share early for a small sum and settled in Carson City where he built the Warm Springs Hotel. This place was first used as a resort. Curry later permitted the Territorial Legislature to meet at the hotel. The Warm Spr-

The Third House, a group of legislators, lawyers and reporters who gathered each evening after legislative sessions and spoofed the daily proceedings. Mark Twain is second from left. Sandy Baldwin is the smaller man in the front row. Mark Twain was elected President of the Third House. *Nevada Historical Society.*

ings Hotel eventually became the Nevada State Penitentiary. Part of the original hotel still exists and can be seen on east Fifth Street. "Old Abe," Curry served as a representative to the second Territorial Legislature and councilman to the third. He was a good friend of Mark Twain's. His many community contributions were were praised by Twain in *Roughing It.*

Thomas Fitch and his wife lived across the hall from Mark Twain and Dan De Quille. Tom Fitch was editor for the Virginia *Daily Union* and later started the short lived, *Occidental,* in March, 1864. Fitch was a journalist, lawyer and a politician noted for his great oratory and dubbed by his friends the "Silver Tongued."

Born in New York, Fitch migrated to California where he worked for newspapers in San Francisco and Placerville. Later admitted to the California bar, Fitch was elected to the California legislature in 1862. Fitch came to Nevada in 1863 and was Storey County delegate to the Constitutional Convention in 1863; served as Washoe City District Attorney 1865-66 and in 1868 was elected to Congress.

James Nye was the first Territorial Governor of Nevada, 1861-64, elected United States Senator from Nevada in 1864 where he served eight years. A rascally politician and clever in his dealing with people, Nye was first a district attorney and judge in Madison County, New York, later president of the Metropolitan Board of Police in New York City.

As Govenor of Nevada Territory, James Nye was boss to Orion Clemens. As the leading politicians, Nye and Orion Clemens were important socially. There were many get togethers and Nye's residence; Mark Twain, Orion and Mollie Clemens and other legislators were regular attendants. Mark Twain admired Nye's political skill and his sense of humor; though Nye was years older, Twain and Nye were good friends. Mark Twain's first speech was in part a satire of Govenor Nye. Governor Nye accepted the satire in stride and later bestowed on Twain one of the coveted notarial commissions. As notary public, Twain was able to earn extra money. Twain gave much space to Governor Nye in *Roughing It.*

Theodore Winters was a sucessful Washoe Valley rancher and farmer. He was a large stock holder in the Ophir Mining Company, owned celebrated race horses and maintained a race track on his ranch. Winters was involved in Territorial politics and was a

Senator William "Bill" Stewart, the rascally attorney who later opened his Washington, D.C. home to Mark Twain where the author wrote, *The Innocents Abroad. Special Collections, University of Nevada, Reno.*

Theodore Winters, Washoe Valley rancher and friend to Mark Twain. Winters and Sandy Baldwin presented Mark Twain with an engraved gold watch as President of the Third House. *Nevada Historical Society.*

member of the Third House. Winters paid half of the $200 for the watch presented to Mark Twain upon his election as President of the Third House. Theodore Winters' house, where Mark Twain often visited, still stands along highway 395 between Carson City and the Virginia City turnoff.

Hal Clayton was the presiding officer of the Third House during the first and second Territorial legislatures. In 1860, he was the prosecuting attorney in Carson City. Like Clemens, Clayton was a southerner and spoke out passionately for the Confederacy. Clayton was arrested by Union soldiers July, 1863 for "persisting in the utterance of disloyal sentiments." Clayton was released and again supervised the Third House proceedings during the 1864, 1867 and 1869 legislative sessions.

Mark Twain frequently mentioned these and other men in his Carson dispatches. Often he made fun of them in his columns. Their willingness to accept public embarrassment in good humor is evidence of their strong friendship and the esteem with which they held Mark Twain.

Mark Twain carefully selected the men with whom he interacted. He preferred educated, successful men with sharp minds who knew how to enjoy themselves. He had a weakness for attorneys and preachers. Both professions employed good talkers and men who possessed a deep commitment to justice. Twain had considered both professions himself. But he could not cope with the legal mumbo-jumbo the law profession required and he never considered himself worthy enough to become a preacher though he enjoyed preaching all sorts of messages throughout his life.

It is surprising Mark Twain chose to associate with such men. All were college educated. Mark Twain was self-conscious about his lack of formal education. He did not finish school and had no more than a seventh grade education. But Twain was a hungry reader and had educated himself by reading the Bible, literature, history and science. Having traveled widely for ten years and worked as a printer, river boat pilot and prospector, Mark Twain met all sorts of people, saw both sides of life and experienced the wide open, real world to its fullest. What he lacked in formal education, he made up in worldly knowledge. Still, there were moments he felt ill at ease because of his lack of education but you would not have suspected it. Twain not only acted as an equal to these men, he

From left to right, Billy Claggett, representative from Humboldt District, an old friend of Mark Twain's, Mark Twain, and Jack Simmons, Speaker of the House.

often outshone them by his wit and attention getting behavior.

Mark Twain now entered his most powerful and prestigious period as journalist for the *Territorial Enterprise*. November 2 the Constitutional Convention convened in Carson City. Mark Twain was there to report. While in Carson City, he again lived with his brother Orion, sister-in-law, Mollie, and his niece, Jennie.

The Convention lasted 32 days and there were 36 delegates. Mark Twain attended each session, made pencil notes in his notebook and afterward wrote a summary of the daily proceedings. Twain was aided by A.J. Marsh, a shorthand expert whom the *Enterprise* had borrowed from the Sacramento *Union*. Though political debates and the dull hours of haggling often bored Twain, he liked the excitment of backroom politicing and enjoyed being in the thick of activity. He enjoyed the commadrie of his old friends Billy Claggett and Jack Simmons. There was a great deal of joking during legislative meetings; afterward members of the Third House gathered in various Carson saloons. A favorite haunt was the Corner Bar at the Ormsby House, Carson's only substantial hotel.

Mark Twain wrote daily dispatches and weekly summaries. The daily reports were dry, factual journalism and were published without a by-line or with "Sam Clemens." The weekly reports written on Sunday were casual and humorous. These contained news about legislative doings, personal comments on legislators and local events and were signed, "Mark Twain". In his autobiography Mark Twain said, "Every Sunday I wrote a letter to the paper [from Carson City] in which I made a resume of the week's legislative work, and in order that it might be readable I put no end of seasoning into it. I signed these letters 'Mark Twain.'" Mark Twain believed it was important to inform readers and equally important for his writing to be entertaining. In his weekly summaries Twain freely gossiped about local characters. Twain understood that people liked reading about other people. He explained this to his sister Pamela in a letter:

Pamela, you wouldn't do for a local reporter--because you don't appreciate the interest that attaches to names. An item is of no use unless it speaks of some person, and not then, unless that person's name is distinctly mentioned. The most interesting letter one can write to an absent freind, is one that treats of persons he has been acquainted with rather than the public events of the day. Now you speak of a young lady who wrote to Hallie Benson that she had seen me, and you didn't mention her name. It was just a mere chance that I ever guessed who she was--but I did finally, though I don't remember her name, now.

March 18, 1864

Mark Twain applied this philosophy in his daily dispatches in which he mentioned more than 250 people.

It was no doubt difficult for Mark Twain to sit through the long, laborious legislative sessions. Mark Twain was a nervous, fidgety person and could not sit still for long. He frequently interupted legislative proceedings but his jokes were taken well by the legislators. January 15, 1864, "The Chair announced Mr. Sam. L. Clemens as entitled to a seat as Reporter for the house, while the courtesy of that body should continue to hold out." Several days later Twain reported, "I am here...on my good behavior, as it were..." Legislators treated Mark Twain as if he were a member of the house rather than a journalist.

Nothing disturbed Mark Twain more than pretentious, windbags. Attending the Constitutional Convention, was a long-winded delegate from Aurora, L.O. Sterns, whom Twain likely knew while in Aurora. Toward the end of the Constitutional Convention, Mark Twain made fun of Sterns' long-winded, wandering speeches:

Mr. Sterns said--Mr. President, I am opposed, I am hostile, I am uncompromisingly against this proposition to tax the mines. I will go further, sir. I will openly assert sir, that I am not in favor of this proposition. It is wrong--entirely wrong...we owe it to our constituents to defeat this pernicious measure. Incorporate it into your Constitution sir,...the gaunt forms of want, poverty, and starvation, and despair will shortly walk in the high places of this once happy and beautiful land. Add it to your fundamental law, sir, and (as was stated yesterday by the gentleman from Lander) God will cease to smile upon your labors. In the language (of my colleague), I entreat you, sir, and gentlemen, inflict not this mighty iniquity upon generations yet unborn! Heed the prayer of the people and be merciful! Ah, sir, the quality of mercy is not strained, so to speak (as has been appropriately suggested heretofore), but droppeth like the gentle dew from Heaven, as it were. The gentleman from Douglas has said this law would be unconstitutional, and I cordially agree with him. Therefore, let its corse to the ramparts be hurried--let the flames that shook the battle's wreck, shine round it o'er the dead--let it go hence to that undiscovered country from whose bourne no traveler returns (as hath been remarked by the gentleman from Washoe, Mr. Shamp), and in this guarding and protecting the poor miner, let us endeavor to do unto others as we would that others should do unto us (as was very justly and properly observed by Jesus Christ upon a former occasion).

The one troubling feature of the newly created state constitution, was a clause which provided for the taxation of mining properties. Mark Twain opposed the measure and feared voters would reject the entire constitution because of it. Bill Stewart went back and forth on the taxation issue. Mark Twain finally took him to task:

...Bill Stewart is always construing something--eternally distorting facts and principles. He would climb out of his coffin and construe the burial service. He is a long-legged, bull headed, whopperjawed, constructionary monomaniac. Give him a chance to construe the sacred law, and there wouldn't be a damned soul in perdition in a month...He construed the Constitution, last night...He gave the public to understand that the clause providing for the taxation of the mines meant nothing in particular; that he wanted the privilege of construing that section to suit himself, that a mere hole in the ground was not a mine, and it wasn't property (he slung that in because he has a costly well on his premises in Virginia); and that it would be a difficult matter to determine in our courts what does really constitute a mine. Do you see his drift? Well, I do. He will prove to the satisfaction of the courts that there are only two definite kinds of mine; that one of these is an excavation from which metallic ores of other mineral substances are "DUG"...Then of course, the miners will know enough to stop "digging" and go to blasting. Bill Stewart will then show, easily enough, that these fellows' claims are not "mines" according to the dictionary, and

consequently cannot be taxed. He will show that the only other species of "mine" is a "pronominal adjective," and that will permit the State to tax the English grammar. He will demonstrate that a mere hole in the ground is not a mine, and is not liable to taxation. The end will be that a year from now we shall all own in these holes in the gound, but no man will acknowledge that he owns in a "mine"; and about that time custom, and policy, and construction, combined will have taught us to speak of the staunch old bulwark of the State as, "The Great Gould & Curry Hole-in-the-Ground"...

Mark Twain's criticism of Stewart may seem exaggerated, but it would not have been unlike Stewart to use such an argument to exempt mines from taxation.

When the state constitution was finally completed, Mark Twain gave his opinion:

...It was an excellent piece of work in some respects, but it had one or two unfortunate defects which debarred it from assuming to be an immaculate conception. The chief of these was a clause authorizing the taxing of the mines. The people will not stand that. There are some 30,000 gold and silver mining incorporations here, or mines, or claims, or which you please, or all, if it suits you better. Very little of the kind of property thus represented is improved yet, or 'developed' as we call it...And until it does begin to pay dividends, the people will not consent that it shall be burdened and hindered by taxation. Therefore, I am satisfied they will refuse to ratify our new constitution on the 19th...

Enterprise, *January 4, 1864*

Twain was right. Voters rejected the state constitition 5 to 1.

Then there was the business of the Great Seal of the State. Twain wrote:

...It had snow-capped mountains in it; and tunnels, and shafts, and pickaxes, and quartz-mills, and pack-trains, and mule-teams. These things were good; what there were of them, And it has railroads in it, and telegraphs, and stars, and suspension bridges, and other romantic fictions foreign to sand and sage-brush. But the richest of it was the motto. It took them thirty days to decide

whether it should be "Volens et Potens" (which they said meant "Able and Willing")...We have an animal here whose surname is the "jackass rabbit". It is three feet long, has legs like a counting-house stool, ears of monstrous length, and no tail to speak of. It is swifter than a greyhound, and as meek and harmless an an infant. I might mention, also, that it is handsome as most infants...Well, somebody proposed as a substitute for that pictorial Great Seal, a figure of a jackass rabbit reposing in the shade of his native sage-brush, with the motto "Volens enough, but not so d---d Potens,"...

Enterprise, *January 4, 1864*

Following the Constitutional Convention the State Nominating Convention met and candidates for bvarious political offices were chosen. Of these political candidates Twain wrote:

...they all owe me something for traducing and vilifying them in the public prints, and thus exciting sympathy for them on the score of persecution, and securing their nomination...I elected those fellows, and I shall take care that I am fairly renumerated for it...

The most striking aspect of Twain's articles during this time, is his empathetic attitude toward issues which affected the community. In "A Gorgeous Swindle," he attacked a fraudulent investment company which was swindling "multitudes of the poorest classes" out of their money. He attacked Bill Stewart for supporting a clause which would have permitted taxation of undeveloped mining properties. Following the death of Orion's daughter, Jennie February 1, Twain lashed out at the sole Carson undertaker who pilfered the pockets of citizens at a time of terrible sorrow and weakness. Twain wrote of this parasite:

There is a system of extortion going on here which is absolutely terrific, and I wonder the Carson Independent has never ventilated the subject. There seems to be only one undertaker in the town, and he owns the only graveyard in which it is at all high-toned or aristocratic to be buried. Consequently, when a man loses his wife or his child, or his mother, this undertaker makes him sweat for it. I appeal to those whose firesides death has made desolate during the few fatal weeks just past, if I am not speaking the truth. Does not this undertaker take advantage of that unfortunate delicacy which prevents a man from disputing an unjust bill for services rendered in burying the dead, to extort ten-fold more than his labors are worth?...This undertaker charges a hundred and fifty dollars for a pine coffin that cost him twenty or thirty, and fifty dollars for a grave that did not cost him ten--and this at a time when his ghastly services are required at least seven times a week...What Carson needs is a few more undertakers--there is vacant land enough here for a thousand cemeteries.

The editor of the Carson *Independent* wrote an editorial response to Twain's article. He denied knowing anything about the undertaker's extortion and wrote that it was the duty of citizens to, "ventilate the matter. We have heard no complaints."

Mark Twain was furious. He lashed out at the incompetent editor:

Having had no use for a coffin himself, the editor "therefore knows nothing about the price of such things." It is my unsolicited opinion that he knows very little about anything. And anybody who will read his paper calmly and dispassionately for a week will endorse that opinion. And more especially his knowing nothing about Carson, is not surprising; he seldom mentions that town in his paper. If the Second Advent were to occur here, you would hear of it first in some other newspaper. He says, "If any of our citizens think they have been imposed upon in this particular, it is their duty to ventilate the matter."...Where did you get your notion of the duties of a journalist from? Any editor in the world will say it is your duty to ferret out these abuses, and your duty to correct them. What are you paid for? What use are you to the community? What are you fit for as conductor of a newspaper, if you cannot do these things. Are you paid to know nothing, and keep on writing about it every day? How long do you suppose such a jack-legged newspaper as your's would be supported or tolerated in Carson, if you had a rival no larger than a foolscap sheet, but with something in it, and whose editor would know, or at least have energy enough to find out, whether a neighboring paper abused one of the citizens justly or unjustly? That paragraph which I have copied, seems to mean one thing, while in reality it means another. Its true translation is, for instance: "Our name is Independent--that is, in different phrase, Opinionless. We have no opinions on any subject--we reside permanently on the fence. In order to have no opinions, it is necessary that we should know nothing--therefore, if this undertaker is fleecing the people, we will not know it, and then we shall not offend him. We have heard no complaints and we shall make no inquiries, lest we do hear some."...

Mr. Curry says if the people will come forward and take hold of the matter, a city cemetery can be prepared and fenced in a week, and at a trivial cost--a cemetery from which a man can set out for Paradise or perdition just as respectable as he can from the undertaker's private grounds at present...

Enterprise, *February 13, 1864*

There were bills and laws Mark Twain apparently lobbied for and against. He was against a telegraph bill which virtually gave one company a monopoly. When another "pet" bill was laid to rest by legislators, Twain took them aside one night:

While I was absent a moment, yesterday, on important business, taking a drink, the House, with its accustomed engaging unanimity, knocked one of my pet bills higher than a kite, without a dissenting voice. I convened the members in extra session last night, and deluged them with blasphemy, after which I entered into a solemn compact with them, whereby, in consideration of their re-instating my bill, I was to make an ample apology for all the mean things I had said about them for passing that infamous, unchristian, infernal telegraph bill the other day. I also promised to apologize for all the mean things that other people had published against them for their depraved action aforesaid. They reinstated my pet today...I hereby solemnly apologize for their rascally conduct in passing the infamous telegraph bill above mentioned. Under ordinary circumstances, they never would have done such a thing--but upon that occasion I think they had been fraternizing with Claggett and Simmons at the White House, and were under the vicious influence of Humboldt whisky. Consequently, they were not responsible...to anybody on earth or in heaven.--Mark Twain

Enterprise, *February 12, 1864*

Twain called the telegraph bill a "monstrosity." As late as April, he complained of the bill's terrible effects:

> *...The infernal telegraph monopoly saddled upon this Territory by the last Legislature, in the passage of that infamous special Humboldt telegraph bill...is bearing its fruits, and the people here, as well as at Virginia, are beginning to wince under illegal and exorbitant telegraphic charges...The moment that law received the Governor's signature last winter, you will recollect the Telegraph Company doubled their prices for dispatches to and from San Francisco. And that is not the worst they have done, if common report be true. This common report says the telegraph is used by its owners to aid them in stock-gambling schemes. I recollect that on the night the jury went out in the Savage and North Potosi case and failed to agree, our San Francisco dispatch failed to come to hand and the reason assigned was that a dispatch of 3,000 words was being sent from Virginia to San Francisco and the line could not be used for other messages. Now that Telegraph Company may have made money by trading in North Potosi on that occasion, but who is young enough to believe they ever got two dollars and a half for that voluminous imaginary dispatch? That telegraph is a humbug...*
> Virginia Evening Bulletin. April 28, 1864

Disturbed by the lack of control the public had over their political representatives, February 16, Mark Twain called for the moving of the Capital from Cason City to Virginia City. He wrote:

> *My first and best reason for thinking the Capital ought to be removed is, that while it remains in Carson, the Legislative Assembly is beyond the pale of newspaper criticism--beyond its restraining influence, and consequently beyond the jurisdiction of the people, in a manner, since the people are left in ignorance of what their servants are doing, and cannot protest against their acts until it is too late. Your reports of proceedings take up as much room in the city papers as can well be spared, I suppose, and they are ample enough for all intents and purposes--or rather, they would be, if the Virginia newspapers could stay in Carson and criticize these proceedings, and also the members, editorially, occasionally. A mere skeleton report carries but an indifferent con-*

ception of the transactions of a Legislative body to the minds of the people. For instance...Mr. Stewart gave notice of a bill entitled an Act to audit the claim of D.J. Gasherie. A day or so afterward, we learn that according to former notice, Mr. Stewart introduced the bill. You hear of it again in some committee report. And again, as having been reported "favorable" by a Committee of the Whole. Next, your report says Mr. Stewart's bill passed by so many ayes, and so many noes. The work is done; none of your readers have the slightest idea what Mr. Gasherie's claim was for...Yet the chief portion of your readers...were very particularly interested in that bill--because they will have to contribute money from their own pockets to pay Mr. Gasherie's claim...Now, if the Legislature had been in session in Virginia, under the eyes of the press, instead of those six or seven idle lobby members, I doubt if Mr. Stewart would have introduced the bill...

Hank Monk, the famous stage driver and friend of Mark Twain's.

Little Jennie Clemens, Orion and Mollie's daughter, who died February 1864. She had been saving her money to buy a large Bible for the First Presbyterian Church.

Grave of Jennie Clemens, Mark Twain's niece, in the Lone Mountain Cemetery, Carson City. Jennie died of Rocky Mountain Spotted fever February, 1864. Her death led to Mark Twain's attack of the sole Carson undertaker who charged exhorbitant prices.

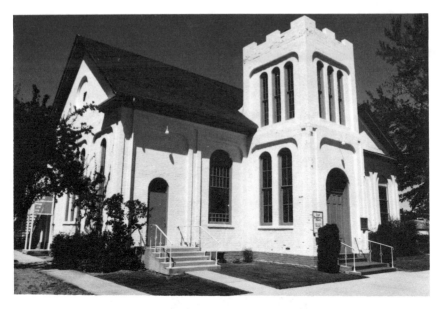

The First Presbyterian Church in Carson City. Mark Twain's first professional lecture was given to raise funds to complete the church. Larry Tanner photo.

Billy Claggett introduced a measure to move the Capital to Virginia City but it was defeated.

In these and other articles, Mark Twain's moralist voice first emerged, a voice that would speak through his writings the rest of his life. It was the deeply compassionate voice of a man able to take ten steps back from the human race, look calmly upon our peculiar behavior and with humor show us ourselves through his unique eyes. Twain's voice had in it the wisdom from another world. Those who had ears to hear, paused and reconsidered their lives, their thoughts, their motivations.

It was a voice of integrity, of a man who knew without question right from wrong, good from evil and went about setting the world straight in his own funny, endearing, sometimes arrogant way. Few were put off by his ranting for Mark Twain readily admitted that he was just as guilty as the rest of us. Of course, that did not stop Twain from telling others what was wrong with their lives or their actions.

Mark Twain was very conscious of his own behavior. He endeavored to be good and responsible; he demanded much of himself and much of others. For all his humor, he took himself and life seriously.

Three things affected his sense of integrity and his morality: his father, his mother and Biblical studies.

From his father, John Clemens, an attorney and judge, Sam inherited a deep sense of justice and integrity. John Clemens was a leading man in his community.

But young Sam Clemens was not close to his father who seemed austere and distant. He was not able to bridge the distance before his father's death when Sam was twelve. One can only guess, but it would seem from the unsatisfying father-son relationship, Sam Clemens may have believed by being good, by being outstanding, that he might win his father's love and approval. This likely led to Clemens' deep need for fame and recognition and his self-demanding nature.

From his mother, Jane Clemens, Sam inherited a profound concern for other people, a need to defend the defenseless. More importantly Jane Clemens, a Bible-reading, hymn singing Christian, taught Sam her own Judaeo-Christian beliefs. This, and Sam's reading and knowledge of the Bible, affected his morality more than anything else.

There is room for argument as to whether or not Mark Twain was religious. Certainly, he was not religious in the ordinary sense. He hated going to church because the sermons often bored him. He claimed he became a Christian before marrying Olivia Langdon but his conversion is questionable. He *was* sincerely drawn to preachers and made great efforts to win their friendship. Joe Twichell, a lifelong friend, was an ordained minister. Mark Twain shared the preachers' sense of justice and love of goodness.

There is no doubt, however, that Mark Twain respected the Bible and believed in its moral teachings. Mark Twain lived in an age where the Bible was taken literally and was the most valued and revered book in the family. The Bible was believed by most Americans to be the Word of God and its moral teachings and values were not questioned. This, in addition to the highly Christian tone of the Victorian era, tremendously affected Mark Twain's morality as it did most men and women.

Other men on the *Enterprise* were equally affected by their Biblical reading and Christian teachings. Dan De Quille, a Quaker, as good a Christian as a man might be, who cared for the downtrodden Piutes, spoke highly of the Bible and revered it. Goodman and

Daggett were equally affected for having read the Bible. Their biblical teachings gave them a fine sense of integrity and justice. They may not have always behaved, but they knew right from wrong.

Mark Twain's early *Enterprise* writings and his first two books, *The Innocents Abroad* and *Roughing It*, contain hundreds of Biblical allusions. Much of Twain's early humor is based on Biblical references and stories. He is continually mentioning the "Almighty," the "Lord," "Heaven and hell," "perdition and Paradise," the "Devil," the "Savior," "life and death," "eternity." These allusions gave breadth and scope to his writing, made the issues he wrote of larger than life. Mark Twain assumed his readers had read the Bible or were familiar with its teachings. Such talk of "Heaven and hell," the "Almighty," instantly gave his writing a moral tone.

Mark Twain while in Virginia City may have been mischievious, may have played practical jokes on his friends, and at times drank too much, but at bottom he was an unhumanly wise, good man. During his long life he won the love, admiration and respect of many fine human beings. Steve Gillis, at a time he believed he was dying in the 1890's said, "Tell Sam I'm going to die pretty soon, but that I love him, and I've loved him all my life and I'll love him till I die." It was a moving tribute for one man to give another.

Mark Twain was good in spite of himself. There was always that conflict in him between good and evil as there is in each of us. How well we win our personal battle to be good determines our individual greatness. Perhaps the battle was stronger in Mark Twain and his efforts to win it are what made him great.

Much of Mark Twain's humor is derived from his self-mockery; he pokes fun at his laziness, calls himself a fool and a liar but resigns himself; for all the good and bad, he is what he is.

On one such occasion when the staff had hidden Mark's candle, a passing minister, Mr. Rising, who later ministered the Episcopal church in Carson City, happened to walk in and caught Mark cursing the thieves who had hidden his candle. Finally Mark turned to Mr. Rising.

"I know, Mr. Rising, I know it's wicked to talk like this; I know it is wrong. I know I shall certainly go to hell for it. But if you had a candle, Mr. Rising, and those thieves should carry it off every night, I know that you would say, just as I say, Mr. Rising, God damn their impenitent souls, may they roast in hell for a million years!"

"Maybe I should, Mr. Clemens, but I should try to say, 'Forgive them, Father, they know not what they do.'"

"Oh, well! if you put it on the ground that they are just fools, that alters the case, as I am one of that class myself. Come in and we'll try to forgive them and forget about it."

Mark Twain's self-mockery and his frankness about his short-comings endears him to readers. He understood there is good and bad in each of us and try as hard as we might, most of us fall short of being as virtuous as we would like.

Thank God, the Almighty, loves us in spite of ourselves.

Jane Clemens, mother of Sam Clemens. She instilled in Sam her strong Christian beliefs and taught him to care for the less fortunate, *Nevada Historical Society.*

CHAPTER THIRTEEN

The Last Good Times

Either in early December or after the legislature finished business February 20, the staff of the *Enterprise* led by that die hard practical joker, Steve Gillis, played the best and worst practical joke on Mark. It happened like this:

From time to time the staff had collected money and presented well regarded staffers with meerschaum pipes. This type of pipe was popular then and expensive, selling anywhere from forty to seventy-five dollars, or several week's wages. The meerschaum had a high bowl which colored when fired-up and a long stem. Mark was disturbed that he had not been presented one and said as much to Steve Gillis.

Steve's wicked brain started cooking and he came up with a plan: they would all get together to present Mark with a *fake* meerschaum pipe. Steve and Dennis McCarthy found an imitation meerschaum at a German cigar store selling for a dollar and a half. They bought the pipe, a three foot cherry stem and a genuine amber mouth-piece. They had a little mounted silver plate engraved, "To Mark Twain, from his Friends."

Then Steve and Dennis went to Dan and asked him to play the part of Judas, "to tell Mark privately that he was going to be presented with a fine pipe, so that he could have a speech prepared." The pipe was to be presented on a Saturday night at Harris' saloon in Maguire's Opera House on D Street "after the paper was up." Charley Pope, then appearing at Maguire's, was let in on the joke and was asked to give the presentation speech. Dan De

Quille later wrote of the affair:

When our victim and all the conspirators had been assembled for some time around the center-table in a private parlor of the saloon, Charley Pope made his appearance. Mark seemed surprised at seeing him enter the room.

Mr. Pope carried under his arm, wrapped in a newspaper a bundle about a yard in length. Advancing to the table he proceeded to unroll the bundle, producing a ridiculous looking pipe, with a straight bowl about five inches high, and about a yard of blue ribbon floating from the stem.

"That is a mighty fine pipe you have there, Charley," said Mark in an off-hand, unconcerned tone of voice.

Mr. Pope made no reply, but throwing the newspaper upon the floor held the pipe aloft by the middle of the stem, as in the great painting of the presentation of the Pipe of Peace, and began his speech with: "Mr. Clemens, on behalf of your friends and admirers, those you see here assembled and many others, I present you this magnificent meerschaum pipe as a slight," etc., etc.

Mr. Pope spoke about twenty minutes, making a really admirable speech. In parts it was very feeling, and again it was witty and jolly. Of course we applauded it from Alpha to Omega.

Then Mark Twain arose...He was sorry that he would be unable fittingly to reply to a speech so able and excellent as that of Mr. Pope--a speech that had touched his heart and stirred in his bosom feelings he could not find words to express...

He then launched forth into what we all knew was his prepared speech. He began with the introduction of tobacco in England by Sir Walter Raleigh, and wound up with George Washington. Just how he managed to bring in the "Father of His Country" I have forgotten; but he had him there in the wind-up...

Reporting With Mark Twain

Steve Gillis continues the story:

...I never felt so sorry for anybody...Still, we were bent on seeing the thing through. After Sam's speech was finished, he ordered expensive wines--champagne and sparkling Moselle. Then we went out to do the town, and kept things going until morning to drown

our sorrow.

Well, next day, of course, he started in to color the pipe. It wouldn't color any more than a piece of chalk, which was about all it was. Sam would smoke and smoke, and complain that it didn't seem to taste right, and that it wouldn't color. Finally Dennis said to him one day:

"Oh, Sam, don't you know that's just a damned old egg-shell, and that the boys bought it for a dollar and a half and presented you with it for a joke?"

Then Sam was furious, and we laid the whole thing on Dan De Quille. He had a thunder-cloud on his face when he started up for the Local Room, where Dan was. He went in and closed the door behind him, and locked it, and put the key in his pocket--an awful sign. Dan was there alone writing at his table.

Sam said, "Dan, did you know, when you invited me to make that speech, that those fellows were going to give me a bogus pipe?"

There was no way for Dan to escape, and he confessed. Sam walked up and down the floor, as if trying to decide which way to slay Dan. Finally he said:

"Oh, Dan, to think that you, my dearest friend, who knew how little money I had, and how hard I would work to prepare a speech that would show my gratitude to my friends, should be the traitor, the Judas, to betray me with a kiss! Dan, I never want to look on your face again. You knew I would spend every dollar I had on those pirates when I couldn't afford to spend anything; and yet you let me do it...you even got me to get up that damned speech to make the thing still more ridiculous."

from Mark Twain In Nevada

Dan tried to calm Mark, by explaining that a new pipe a real meerschaum had been ordered and would arrive soon. Mark was not easily appeased. When the real meerschaum was delivered and given to Mark, he told Steve Gillis, "I think that bogus pipe smokes about as well as the good one."

Years later when Joe Goodman visited Mark in Hartford he said to Goodman, "...that was a cruel, cruel trick the boys played on me; but, for the feeling I had during the moment when they presented me with that pipe and when Charley Pope was making his speech and I was making my reply to it--for the memory of that feeling, now, that pipe is more precious to me than any pipe in the world!"

When angry, Mark Twain expressed himself, either verbally or by throwing something. Tom Fitch, who lived across the hall from Mark and Dan, recalled that whenever something went wrong for Mark, he had the habit of crashing plates and making a disturbing racket.

Tom told the story of a practical joke he and Rollin Daggett played on Mark the Christmas of 1863 which culminated in Mark's making use of the dinner dishes.

Tom and Rollin Daggett were in the smoking-room waiting for dinner when a messenger boy arrived with a package for Mark. Tom Fitch explains what happened next:

...After his departure we examined the bundle, for we were communists in spirit, and found that it contained a pretty knitted woolen scarf and a card bearing the inscription, "Mr. Samuel L. Clemens, from his friend Etta." "I can improve on that message," suggested Daggett, who was the wag and philosophical disputant and cribbage player of the club, and, obtaining a sheet of note paper, he wrote in a fine female hand the following note:

"Mr. Clemens: The accompanying scarf having been prepared as a Christmas gift for you, it has been determined not to divert it from its original destination, although a knowledge of your late conduct having come to the ears of the writer your own conscience will tell you that this must close all communication between us, in which decision my father and mother concur. Your former friend, 'Etta.'"

The scarf was rewrapped and with this note tied to it was placed in Sam's room. Shortly afterward he made his appearance and proceeded to his room to prepare for dinner. Soon we heard the crockery going. "What is the matter, Sam?" said Daggett. Thereupon entered Mark Twain, with the coat and collar off, and throwing the package upon the table, burst forth: "Read that. That's just my infernal luck. You hounds can run the town night after night and nobody ever says a word, but I am found out at once."

Western Carpetbagger

Fitch spoke highly of Twain's integrity, "...he was free from the vices of a frontier community and an honorable and upright man in his dealings--except in one particular. He was the most accomplished midnight mince pie thief that ever upset the calculations of our widow caterer [Fitch's mother-in-law]."

A popular sporting place for young Comstock men during 1863-64 was a fencing school and gymnasium ran by M. Chauvel, a French restaurant keeper. Mark Twain, Joe Goodman and Dan De Quille for a time were fencing fanatics. Mark Twain became an expert and was a fiery and dangerous opponent because, as Dan De Quille put it, one could not see his eyes which were habitually worn half closed.

Chauvel kept on hand boxing gloves for those who wished to box: Steve Gillis, Dennis McCarthy, George Dawson and several others preferred boxing to fencing. Dawson was the best *Enterprise* boxer and he took pride in being a hard hitter. Dennis McCarthy was the only one who would fight Dawson and their sparring matches always ended in an angry battle for blood.

One day Mark Twain was encouraged by some imp to try on the boxing gloves. He began dancing around the hall flinging punches into the air, fooling around, Dan De Quille tells what happened next:

> *Presently Mark squared off directly in front of Dawson and began working his right like the piston of a steam engine, at the same time stretching out his neck and gyrating his curly pate in a very astonishing manner.*
>
> *Dawson took this to be a direct act of defiance--a challenge to a trial of skill that could not be ignored. Desperately, therefore, and probably not without a seret chill of heart, Dawson drew off and with full force planted a heavy blow squarely upon Mark's offered nose, the latter not making the least movement toward a guard. The force of the blow fairly lifted Mark off his feet and landed him across a settle that stood against the wall on the side of the hall, when Dawson, flushed with victory, ran up and, against all rules, began punching him in the head.*
>
> *Dawson was hauled off by McCarthy, Gillis and others and was sternly rebuked. There was a plentiful flow of claret and oaths as Mark staggered to his feet and began looking for a club. He assured Dawson that the next time he undertook to entertain him it would be with a dray-pin.*

With a hand and a handkerchief screening his wounded nose,
Mark...took his departure for our rooms on B Street, leaving a trail
of blood across the hall, up the stairs, through the restaurant above
and all along his homeward route. His nose streamed blood.

An hour later I found him in our little parlor planted in front of a
looking-glass. All the remainder of the day he sat there and tender-
ly ministered to the wants of his ailing nose.

San Francisco Examiner, *March 19, 1893*

The next day Mark had a black eye and a swollen red nose. Ashamed of what had happened, he would not venture outside during the day and snuck down to the *Enterprise* offices at night. One evening Little Deane, a printer caught a glimpse of Mark's nose and cried out, "Why Mr. Clemens, what is the matter with your nose? It looks like an egg-plant!"

"Get out of here, blast you, or I'll make you look like a corpse! No printer has a damn bit of right to come into this room, copy or no copy!" Little Deane scurried back to the print shop.

Hoping to escape the ridicule from those Mark had insulted in his columns, Mark left for Silver Mountain to report the new mines. No sooner was he gone, when Dan wrote a humorous article about Mark's arrival in Silver Mountain. Upon catching a glimpse of Mark's nose, Silver Mountain residents cried out that a "freak" show had come to town. People dropped everything and flocked to the stage, trying to get a look at Mark's nose. They asked the driver if the nose was real and when and where the show would be. They cheered the nose as it stepped from the stage.

It was typical *Enterprise* joking but Mark was furious and told De Quille, "it wasn't a damn bit smart." The Carson bums hounded him when he arrived there until he was forced to threaten them to shut their mouths.

A few days later Dan was thrown from a horse and sprained his knee. The accident offered Mark the opportunity to get back at Dan. Twain wrote an exaggerated account, "Frightful Accident to Dan De Quille."

Our time honored confrere, Dan, met with a disastrous acci-
dent, Tuesday, while returning from American City on a vicious
Spanish horse...Dan was wrenched from his saddle and thrown

some three hundred yards...alighting upon solid ground, and bursting himself open from the chin to the pit of the stomach; his head was also caved in out of sight, and his hat was afterward extracted in a bloody and damaged condition from between his lungs; he must have bounced end-for-end after he struck first, because it is evident he received a concussion from the rear that broke his heart; one leg was jammed up in his body nearly to his throat, and the other was so torn and mutilated that it pulled out when they attempted to lift him into the hearse which we had sent to the scene of the disaster, under the general impression that he might need it; both arms were indiscriminately broken up until they were jointed like bamboo; his back was considerably fractured and bent into the shape of a rail fence. Aside from these injuries, however, he sustained no other damage...Our noble old friend is recovering fast, and what is left of him will be around the breweries again today, just as usual.

Dan De Quille was well known on the Coast. When Mark's story was published in the *Enterprise* and re-printed in other Coast papers, there was real concern for Dan's health. Worse, the *Enterprise* was received by Dan's wife in Iowa and she was horror stricken when she read the story.

But Mark was happy. He chuckled at Dan, "Now, blast you, maybe you'll hereafter let my nose alone!"

February 27, Adah Isaacs Menken, then a leading American actress, arrived from San Francisco with her poor, ignored husband, Orpheus Kerr trailing behind her along with a company of actors, friend Ada Clare and a pack of dogs. Menken was best know for her performance in *Mazeppa*, a drama based on Byron's poem. She acquired fame in the climatic scene in which she was disrobed in full view of the audience and was left wearing flesh colored tights to simulate nudity. In San Francisco, she replaced the tights with a short skirt. This, for that time, was outlandish. Needless to say, the Menken's strip act was popular with men and audiences roared with approval. Even critics liked her, except for Mark Twain.

While in San Francisco in September, 1863, Mark Twain caught her act at Maguire's Opera House. September 13, he wrote the *Enterprise*:

When I arrived in San Francisco, I found there was no one in town--or least there was no body in town but "the Menken"--or rather , that no one was being talked about except that manly young female. I went to see her play "Mazeppa," of course. They said she was dressed from head to toe in flesh-colored "tights," but I had no opera-glass, and I couldn't see it, to use the language of the inelegant rabble. She appeared to me to have but one garment on-- a thin tight white linen one, of unimportant dimensions; I forget the name of the article, but it is indispensable to infants of tender age--I suppose any young mother can tell you what it is...With the exception of this superfluous rag, the Menken dresses like the Greek Slave; but some of her postures are not so modest as the suggestive of the cavorting around after "Olinska"; she bends herself back like a bow; she pitches headforemost at the atmosphere like a battering-ram; she works her arms, and her legs, and her whole body like a dancing-jack: her every movement is as quick as thought; in a word, without any apparent reason for it, she carries on like a lunatic from the beginning of the act to the end of it. At other times she "wallops" herself down on the stage, and rolls over as does the sportive pack-mule after his burden is removed. If this be grace then the Menken is eminently graceful. After a while they proceed to strip her, and the high chief Pole calls for the "fiery untamed steed"; a sobordinate Pole brings in the fierce brute...They strap Mazeppa on his back, fore and aft, and face uppermost the horse goes cantering up-stairs over the painted mountains, through the tinted clouds of theatrical mist, in a brisk exciting way, with the wretched victim he bears unconsciously digging her heels into his hams, in the agony of her sufferings, to make him go faster. Then a tempest of applause bursts forth, and the curtain falls...The "French Spy" was played last night and the night before, and as this spy is a frisky Frenchman, and as dumb as an oyster, Miss Menken's extravagant gesticualtions do not seem so overdone in it as they do in "Mazeppa." She don't talk well, and as she goes on her shape and her acting, the character of a fidgety "dummy" is peculiarly suited to her line of business. She plays the Spy, without words, with more feeling than she does Mazeppa with them...

The Menken appeared at Maguire's Opera House in Virginia City. The first night she performed the "French Spy" but it did not go over well. The next night the Menken performed *Mazeppa* and the audience went ape. Her strip act was awarded with a $2,000 bar of silver.

The Menken partied in Virginia City for about a month. She loved the town. She visited the saloons, hurdy houses, gambling houses and brothels often accompanied by Tom Peasely, the owner of the Sazerac saloon, the fire chief and political boss. Mark Twain's, character in *Roughing It*, Buck Fanshaw, was based on Peasely who was murdered shortly after in a Carson City saloon.

Menken had an ego as big as the moon and vanity to match. She thought herself a poet and novelist. Some of her poems were published in the *Golden Era* and in the *Enterprise* during her visit.

One evening she invited Mark Twain and Dan De Quille to a dinner party at her rooms at the International Hotel to discuss her literary future. The only guests were Dan, Mark, Ada Clare, the Menken and her pack of dogs. Menken did not invite her husband, Orepheus Kerr, apparently in the dog house, so to speak, who paced back and forth in the hall outside occasionally sticking his head through the door to scowl at the festivities. The situation made Mark and Dan uncomfortable. Dan later wrote of Menken's dinner party:

> *The object of the dinner appeared to be, on Menken's part, a sort of literary consultation. She was full of her proposed novel. Aside from this talk, and some talk of getting up a new play for Clare, the dinner was rather dull. It was thought to enliven the occasion with...song...but the Menken was no nightingale, Clare was a sort of wren, and I was a screech owl. Mark enchanted us with his one and only song of:*
>
> > *There was an old horse and his name was Jerusalem.*
> > *And he came from Jerusalem,*
> > *And he went to Jerusalem.*
> > *There was an old horse...*
>
> *And so on* ad infinitum.
>
> *In the room were about ninteen dogs of as many breeds, "mongrel, puppy, whelps and hound, and curs of low degree," some Ada Clare's pets and others belonging to the Menken. These*

pampered beasts the pair continually fed upon cubes of sugar soaked in brandy and champagne. This provender made the animals howlingly hilarious, to the great delight of their mistress, but to the disgust of Twain, who was seated on Menken's side of the table, where the canine carnival was most rampant.

Presently one of the dogs took an unwanted liberty with Mark's leg. Guessing at the whereabouts of the cur under the table, Mark undertook to avenge the nip he had received with a sly kick. He missed the dog but hit the Menken's pet corn, causing her to bound from her seat, throw herself on a lounge and roll and roar in agony.

This mischance put a sort of damper on the festivities. Mark immediately became sullen as if it had been his own corn that was wounded, and even when Menken came limping back to her chair and begged him not to mind, he refused to be conciliated.

Mark disliked the Menken and would have avoided the arrangement that seated him by her side had it been possible.

...Mark...soon imagined a pressing engagement and begged to be excused...Thus tamely and unsatisfactorily ended our big dinner.

Adah Isaacs Menken, the actress, whose, "Mazeppa," brought the house down in Virginia City. Mark Twain was not impressed. *Special Collections University of Nevada, Reno.*

Tom Peasley, proprietor of the Sazarac Saloon and Virginia City fire chief. Mark Twain's, Buck Fanshaw character in *Roughing It,* was based on Peasley. Peasley was gunned down February 2, 1866 in the Corner Saloon of the Ormsby House by Martin Barnhart. *Special Collections, University of Nevada, Reno.*

Shortly after her visit to Virginia City, the Menken left her husband for a horse trainer whom she had met in Virginia City. She died in Paris, June, 1868.

Ada Clare was bitten by her pet dog January 30, 1874 and died of hydrophobia.

March 18, Mark wrote to his sister Pamela:

Joe Goodman is gone to the Sandwich Islands. I stipulated, when I took his place, that I should never be expected to write editorials about politics or eastern news. I take no interest in those matters. I wanted to go with Joe, but the news-editor was expecting every day to get sick (he has since accomplished it,) & we could not all leave at once.

Mark Twain was now the *Enterprise's* chief editor. Joe Goodman, like Orion years before, had left the paper in the charge of a prankster who was about to get the *Enterprise* and himself into some serious mischief.

CHAPTER FOURTEEN

Mark Twain Leaves Virginia City

As spring returned to the mountains, Virginia City was noticeably quieter. The first great boom had subsided. Violent crimes were down; there was an unusual calm. Some believed the flush times were over, many had left town.

With little news to report, Mark Twain relied on his fertile imagination to fill his columns. This time his victim was Tom Fitch, editor for the Virginia *Union* who lived across the hall from Mark and Dan. April 1, 1864, the Virginia *Evening Bulletin* reported:

> *Mark Twain, who is notorious for constantly lying...made another mistake by perpetuating the following supposed-to-be sensational item as a goak, [joke] but we can't for the life of us see where the laugh comes in.*
>
> *ANOTHER TRAITOR.--HANG HIM!--The following complaint was yesterday made in the Court of Judge Davenport, by Mr. Thomas Fitch...*
>
> *Thomas Fitch...said that W. F. Meyers did, on the 30th March, 1864, in the office of Myers & Daggett, in the city of Virginia, use the following language, "That he...did not believe that a negro was the equal of a white man, that negros were inferior to white men, and were designed by God Almighty to be the servants of white men, and defendant also used other language derogatory of the character of our fellow-citizens of African descent, and calculated to damnify them and bring them into contempt and ridicule...by*

said slanderous language the colored race aforesaid were greatly
scandalized, and the Government of the United States brought into
disrepute and the Southern Confederacy encouraged, and Uncle
Abe greatly maligned...this complainant prays that a warrant may
issue against the defendant for misprision of treason, and that
defendant's body be taken into custody, and that defendant be
punished either by hanging, or by being compelled to pack sand-
bags at Fort Churchill...

Of course, Tom Fitch never made this complaint against Myers, a friend who owned the Myers and Daggett building where Tom Fitch and his family lived. Mark meant the story as an April Fool's Day joke. Fitch probably took it well but the Virginia *Evening Bulletin* believed using slavery and partisan loyalties was going too far for a joke. America was in the middle of the Civil War; partisan loyalties and slavery were sensitive issues even way out West in Virginia City.

The *Bulletin* concluded its attack of the Fitch joke with, "We suppose our neighbor [Twain] thinking because this is April Fool's Day, he had a greater license than usual. But we don't see it. He who is fool all the rest of the year, has no special rights on this particular day.'

Mark was angered by the *Bulletin's* comments and wrote a pointed response published in the next day's *Enterprise*; the item has since been lost. The next day the *Bulletin* responded to Mark's inability to accept what he dished out:

Sammy Clemens, or as he styles himself, Mark Twain, scribbles
the funny things...for the Enterprise, *and is not a little addicted to*
saying hard things about others, as he pretends, in joke, appears to
feel it intensely when others turn the joke on him. No man living
loves a joke better than ourselves, and we are always as ready to
take as to make one. Sammy, it appears, is differently constituted
to us in this respect. Perhaps he imagines because he is Sammy,
that he has a right to do what others with less pretentions to the
character of wit...have not...Merciless himself in perpetrating
jokes on others, he winces like a cur with a flea in his ear when
others retort; showing conclusively that he has quite misconceived
that nature of the character he had assumed--that of being

Washoe's wit!

The *Bulletin* weeks later called Twain, "an ass of prodigious ear, and a malicious and illiterate cuss generally." But the *Bulletin* was forgiving; April 28, the paper reprinted Mark's condemnation of the new telegraph law.

Mark Twain was nearing the end of his career on the *Enterprise*. It was springtime and with spring, Twain later wrote, "I grow restless, I get the fidgets; I want to pack off somewhere where there's something going on." Virginia City was clearly slowing down, finding stories to fill his columns was becoming a chore. Mark Twain was tired of being in one place for so long.

In a matter of several weeks he created difficulties for himself which eventually led to his departure from Virginia City. It happened like this:

Mark received a request from his sister, Pamela, to raise donations for the St. Louis Sanitary Fair. The United States Sanitary Fund was a forerunner of the American Red Cross, a privately funded organization which aided soldiers in various ways: inspected the camps, provided transportation for the sick and wounded, helped needy families of soldiers, published pamphlets aimed at improving camp sanitation. Large cities held Sanitary Fairs to raise money for the organization.

Inspired by Pamela's suggestion, Twain wrote several editorials supporting the Sanitary Fund hoping to stimulate enthusiasm but Virginia showed little interest. Twain organized a meeting at Maguire's Opera House and managed to raise a slim $580. His friend, Paul, got the ladies of Gold Hill to give a ball and they raised $3,000 which they donated in the form of a silver brick. Twain and his comrades were about to give up on the Sanitary Fund when Ruel Gridley arrived with his sack of flour.

Ruel Gridley was an old schoolmate of Twain's, then living in Austin, a mining town in eastern Nevada Territory. Gridley had hit upon a unique way of earning money for the Sanitary Fund. It began with the loss of a bet. Gridley made a bet on the outcome of a local election. The loser was to carry a fifty pound sack of flour one mile to the next town. Gridley lost the bet and carried the flour sack to the next town where he suggested the sack of flour be autioned off and the proceeds donated to the Sanitary Fund. Gridley succeeded in selling the sack of flour for $5300! It was such a successful means of raising donations, that Gridley decided to take the flour sack to other Nevada towns.

Mark Twain teamed with Gridley when he arrived in Virginia City. Twain wrote his mother and sister May 16 and told them what followed:

...Ruel got here yesterday, with his sack, on his way to the States. Paul thought we might make some use of it. We put it up at auction and it only brought five or six hundred dollars. He lives in Gold Hill, and he said he was so disgusted with Virginia that he would try his own town, and if she failed he would leave the country. This morning at eleven o'clock he had two open carriages--one for reporters and the other for the speakers--got a brass brand and we started for Gold Hill. When we got there Ruel gave the history of the flour sack, and said that from what he could see people outside of Austin didn't care much for flour, but they soon made him small. Gold Hill raised Austin out of her boots, and paid nearly seven thousand dollars in gold for the sack of flour. Ruel threw up the sponge!

Then we went down to little Silver City and sold it for $1,500 or $1,700. From there we went to the village of Dayton and sold it for somewhere in the neighborhood of $2,000...we started home again about $10,000 better off than when we left in the morning.

We got to Gold Hill at 4 in the afternoon, and found the streets crowded, and they hailed us from all sides with "Virginia's boomin'!" "Virginia's mad!" "Virginia's got her back up!" "You better go 'long to Virginia; they say they'll be d--d if the whole Territory combined shall beat them!"...we journeyed into Virginia with a long procession at our heels, coming to see the fun. We got to the meeting place after dark, and found the neighboring buildings illuminated and the adjacent streets completely blocked with people. Then the fun commenced, and I wished Pamela could have been there to see her own private project bringing forth its fruit...for if she had not written us, the St. Louis Fair would probably have never heard from Washoe. She has certainly secured $30,000 or $40,000 worth of greenbacks from us by her own efforts.

Well, the fun commenced...In two hours and a half Virginia *cleaned out the Territory and paid nearly $13,000 for the sack of flour!...Nearly a dollar a head for every man, woman and child in the camp, in two hours and a half; and on four hours notice...*

The other day the Daily Union *gave $200 and I gave $300, [for the* Enterprise*] under instruction from the proprietors [Goodman and McCarthy] always to "go them a hundred better." To-night the* Union *bid $100, and I bid $150 for the* Enterprise. *I had to go to the office to make up my report, and the* Union *fellows came back and bid another $100. It was provoking, because I had order to run our bid up to $1,000, if necessary, and I only struck the* Union *light to draw them on. But I guess we'll make them hunt their holes yet, before we are done with them.*

The Gridley procession was a great celebration and there was much beer drinking along the way. The *Old Piute* wrote:

...we are requested... to make an estimate of the amount of lager beer drank by Marshall, of the Union, *Clemens, of the* Enterprise, *and Gillespie, of the* Old Piute, *while on their travels with that sack...the amount consumed by the three gentlemen above mentioned, is as follows: Paid for by the above reporters, 1 quart; paid for by the public--a sufficient quantity to make Clemens good natured, Marshall communicative and Gillespie to get into our bed with his boots on, and attempt to say the Lord's prayer.*

Gridley afterward sold the sack in Carson City, Sacramento and San Francisco. He carried the sack east where he sold it in several large cities. By the time he reached the St. Louis Sanitary Fair, Gridley and his sack of flour had raised $150,000 for the Sanitary Fund.

The Gridley flour sack procession began a drinking spree for Mark and Dan which lasted several days. The procession had stopped at numerous watering holes along their route. By the time Mark and Dan reached Virginia City they were plowed although their inebriated state did not seem to interfere with their reporting.

One evening shortly afterward, Mark and Dan, half-lit from another day of celebrating, were putting the paper to bed when Mark remembered something he overheard someone in the crowd say as to why the flour sack was not taken to Carson: money raised at the Sanitary Fancy Dress Ball by the Carson ladies had been misappropriated and sent to the Miscegenation Society and it was feared other funds raised in Carson would meet a similar fate. "Miscegenation," which meant the blending of the black and white races was a contoversial theory spawned by an anonymous pamphlet which suggested intermarriage as a solution to the race problem in America. The Miscegenation Society was created to promote this idea.

Mark Twain had no evidence to prove that funds raised by the Carson ladies had been sent to the Miscegenation Society. But he wrote up the item as a joke not intending it for publication but mistakenly left it on the writing table where a printer found it and the next day it was published in the *Enterprise*.

When the item appeared in the *Enterprise*, the Carson ladies wrote a letter to the editor. They denied the charges set forth in the article, demanded to know who the writer was and asked for an apology. When Mark learned of the error, he wrote Mollie Clemens in Carson, May 20:

> ...that item about the sack of flour slipped into the paper without either my consent or Dan's. We kept that Sanitary spree up for several days, and I wrote and laid that item before Dan when I was not sober (I shall not get drunk again, Mollie,)--and said he, "Is this a joke?" I told him "Yes." He said he would not like such a joke as that to be perpetrated upon him, and that it would wound the feelings of the ladies of Carson. He asked me if I wanted to do that, and I said "No, of course not," and I threw it on the table. While we were talking, the manuscript lay on the table, and we forgot it and left it there when we went to the theatre, and I never thought of it again until I received this letter tonight, for I have not read a copy of the Enterprise for a week. I suppose the foreman, prospecting for copy, found it, and seeing that it was in my handwriting, thought it was to be published and carried it off.
>
> Now Mollie, whatever blame there is , rests with me alone...Since it has made the ladies angry, I am sorry the thing occurred, and that is all I can do, for you will see yourself that their communication is altogether unanswerable. I cannot...explain it by saying the affair was a silly joke, and that I and all concerned were drunk. No--I'll die first.

...Either satisfy those ladies that I dealt honorably by them... or else make them appoint a man to avenge the wrong done them, with weapons in fair and open field.

They will understand at a glance that I cannot submit to the humiliation of publishing myself as a liar...

Mollie, the Sanitary expedition has been disastrous to me. Aside from this trouble...I have two other quarrels on my hands, engendered on that day, and as yet I cannot tell how either of them is to end...

Mollie Clemens, Orion's wife. *Nevada Historical Society.*

May 24, Mark Twain published an apology to the Carson ladies. His apology was accepted but one woman's husband, Mr. Cutler wanted Mark's head and wrote a threatening letter. Mark responded with a hot reply telling Cutler if he wasn't content with his apology to challenge him. But after showing the letter to Dan, Mark wrote a less volatile letter which did not lead to violence.

Now, as if Mark Twain did not have enough on his hands, he started more trouble. Joe Goodman was away, Mark was in charge. He took it upon himself to write a scathing editorial, "How Is It?--How It Is," in which he criticized the Virginia *Union* for what he considered its ungenerouus support of the Sanitary Fund. This began a series of letters back and forth between Mark and James Laird, owner of the *Union*. The hostiities reached a pitch when Twain called Laird, "an unmitigated liar," and challenged him to a duel. Dueling and challenges to duel were against the law.

After insulting the ladies of Carson and making a fool of himself by his hostile, petty letter to Laird, Mark Twain was in disfavor. Jerry Driscoll, friend, former *Enterprise* partner, and grand jury foreman, warned Mark that he would be arrested if he did not leave town.

Mark and Steve Gillis packed and prepared to leave. May 26 Mark wrote Orion:

> *Send me two hundred dollars if you can spare it comfortably.--However, never mind--you can send it to San Francisco if you prefer. Steve and I are going to the States. We leave Sunday morning per Henness Pass. Say nothing about it, of course. We're not afraid of the grand jury, but Washoe has long since grown irksome to us, and we want to leave it anyhow.*
> *...we dare not do anything, either to Laird or Carson men without spoiling our chances of getting away. However, if there is any chance of the husbands of those women challenging me I don't want a straw put in the way of it. I'll wait for them a month, if necessary, and fight them with any weapon they choose. I thought of challenging one of them and then crossing the line to await the result, but Steve says it would not be safe, situated as we are...*

May 29, Mark and Steve Gillis left Virginia City by stage. Steve Gillis recalled:

...when the stage left next morning for San Francisco we were on the outside seat. Joe Goodman had returned by this time and agreed to accompany us as far as Henness Pass. We were all in good spirits and glad we were alive, so Joe did not stop when he got to Henness Pass, but kept on. Now and then he would say, "Well, I had better be going back pretty soon," but went with us clear to San Francisco, and we had a royal good time all the way. I never knew any series of duels to close so happily.

Upon Mark Twain's departure from Virginia City, the Gold Hill *News* wrote:

Among the few immortal names of the departed - that is, those who departed yesterday per California stage--we notice that of Mark Twain. We don't wonder, Mark Twain's beard is full of dirt, and his favor is black before the people of Washoe. Giving way to the idiosyncratic eccentricities of an erratic mind, Mark has indulged in the game infernal--in short, "played hell." Shifting the local of his tales of fiction from the Forest of Dutch Nick's to Carson City; the dramatis personae thereof from the Hopkins family to the fair Ladies of the Sanitary Fair; and the plot thereof from murder to miscegenation--he slopped. The indignation aroused by his enormities has been too crushing to be borne by living man, though sheathed with the brass and triple cheek of Mark Twain.
May 30, 1864

A week later the Gold Hill *News* wrote:

The newspaper maker is not regarded by the popular eye as the compiler of "News," but as the manufacturer of that great staple of popular pabulum. Such manufacturers, there be in the world, and such as one did upon a time abide in Washoe; but that man has disappeared from the land and has we fear disappeared from our gaze forever. Is it necessary to say that we allude to the lamented Twain? That loved and lost journalist, tortured by demand for "news" when it was not, did manufacture some that he fondly believed would satisfy the public craving. He filled the pine forest at Dutch Nick's with the ghastly corpses of the Hopkins family and sprinkled the road to Carson with gore from the vermillion scalp of

177

the apocryphal mother of those mythical slain. That "news" satisfied the greedy mind of the public...But mark the sequel: the indignation of the nonmanufacturer and the diabolical damnation of the deceived. The fate of that unhappy man is before us, and warns us to avoid the rock upon which he split...

June 8, 1864

The *Old Piute*, however, was more forgiving and wrote:

Left yesterday for bluer skies and more verdant hills, S.L. Clemens. Esq., alias "Mark Twain". Yes, Mark has gone, and amid our fragrant sage brush, quartz-crowned hills and alkali hydrants we repose solitary and almost alone. The world is blank-- the universe worth but 57 1/2, and we are childless. We shall miss Mark; his bosom friend De Quille will miss him; Marshal will do ditto; every lunch house in the city, every brewery and every woman (who knew him)--and to know was to love him - will miss him. We can't dwell on this subject; we can only say--God bless you, Mark! be virtuous and happy.

June 11, 1864

In San Francisco, Mark and Steve went to work for the San Francisco *Call*. Mark contributed articles to the *Golden Era* and wrote correspondent letters for the *Enterprise* from October, 1865 to March, 1866. In San Francisco, his reputation as a journalist and celebrity grew.

Following trouble with the San Francisco police, Twain escaped to Jim Gillis' cabin on Jackass Hill near Sonora where he heard the story of the jumping frog. The publication of the "The Celebrated Jumping Frog of Calaveras County," in 1865 won Mark Twain national reknown.

A trip to the Sandwich (Hawaiian) Islands in 1866 led Twain to scoop the sinking of the *Hornet* and the rescue of its survivors. Twain's *Hornet* series solidified his West Coast reputation.

When Twain returned to San Francisco, he presented his first lecture based on his visit to the Sandwich Islands. The lecture was a great success. Mark hired Dennis McCarthy as his manager and the two presented the lecture in Sacramento, Grass Valley and other Sierra mining camps.

October 27, Mark Twain arrived in Virginia City with McCarthy to present his Sandwich Island lecture. The evening of October 31, Piper's Opera House was crammed. Twain's hour and a half lecture brought the house down. The prodigal son was welcomed home.

Twain lectured at Dayton, November 7, Silver City, the 9th and Gold Hill, the 10th.

The Odeon Hall Saloon in Dayton where Mark Twain drank and played billiards. Mark Twain may have presented a lecture here in November, 1866.

While returning from his Gold Hill lecture with McCarthy, Mark Twain encountered his last practical joke instigated by who else, Steve Gillis. As Mark and Dennis crossed the Divide, a notorious hold-up site, six men approached in the darkness. Mark Twain reported next day in the *Enterprise* that the men accosted them. The leader, a small man, said:

"Stand and deliver!"

I said, "My son, your arguments are powerful. Take what I have, but uncock that infamous pistol."

The young man uncocked the pistol (but he requested three other gentleman to present theirs at my head) and then he took all the money I had (only $20 or $25) and my watch. Then he said to one of his party:

"Beauregard, go through that man!" meaning Mac--and the distinguished rebel did go through Mac. Then the little captain said:

"Stonewall Jackson, seat these men by the roadside and hide yourself; if they move within five minutes, blow their brains out!"

"All right, sir!" said Stonewall. Then the party (six in number) started toward Virginia City and disappeared.

What bothered Mark most was the theft of his gold watch. The following day he published a plea in the *Enterprise*:

Now I want to write you road agents as follows: My watch was given me by Judge Sandy Baldwin and Theodore Winters, and I value it above anything else I own. If you will send that to me (to the Enterprise *office or to any prominent man in San Francisco), you may keep the money and welcome. You know, you got all the money Mac had--and Mac is an orphan--and besides, the money he had belonged to me. Adieu, my romantic friends.*

Dan De Quille later wrote of the robbery:

The robbery had been planned by Mark's old friends as a sort of advertising dodge. It was intended to create sympathy for him, and by having him deliver a second lecture in Virginia City afford the people an opportunity of redeeming the good name of the Com-

stock. He would have had a rousing benefit, and after all was over his agent would have returned his watch and money. Of course it would not have done to ask Mark his consent to be robbed for this purpose...His friends meant well, but like other schemes of mice and men this particular one failed to work. Mark was too "hot" to be handled and when at last it was explained to him that the robbery was a sham affair he became still hotter--he boiled over with wrath.

His money and watch were returned to him after he had taken his seat in the stage, and his friends begged him to remain, but he refused to disembark. Upon observing some of his friends of the police force engaged in violent demonstrations of mirth, he turned his attention to them and fired a broadside of anathemas as the stage rolled away. Had he kept cool he would have had a benefit that would have put at least a thousand dollars in his pocket, for the papers had made a great sensation of the robbery.

Reporting With Mark Twain

Shortly after, Mark lectured at Washoc City where he stayed several days with Tom Fitch and his family. Tom recalled a conversation which shows Mark Twain's insecurity regarding his talent and his practical mindedness. Following Mark's lecture Fitch said:

He [Mark Twain] was exceedingly nervous about it and though it was received by the audience with laughter and applause he was undoubtedly not quite satisfied with the result.

"Now tell me honestly," said he, "for I want criticism and not praise, what do you think of it?"

"Sam," said I, "as a humorous writer you have no equal, and you will speedily take rank, both here and in the Atlantic states, as the first in the land."

"But, as a lecturer," he said, "now tell me the truth honestly--as a lecturer I am a fraud, am I not?"

"You are," I answered.

"I suspected as much," said he gloomily, "but I'll tell you what it is, there are over 500 towns in the United States of more than 5000 inhabitants, and I can play them all once."

Western Carpetbagger

Mark Twain left California by ship December 13, 1866. After a visit to the Holy Land in the summer of 1867, he returned to New York, then settled in Washington, D.C. There in the fall he began work on his first book, *The Innocents Abroad*, based on letters he wrote for the *Alta California*. When it appeared the *Alta* would not release rights to the letters, Mark Twain was forced to make a trip to California in March, 1868 in order to secure them.

To earn money, Twain gave lectures in San Francisco and other towns. On his way to Virginia City to deliver his Holy Land lecture, Mark wired ahead, "I am doing well, having crossed one divide without getting robbed anyway. Mark Twain," which showed he had forgiven his friends their transgressions.

April 24, he arrived in Virginia City for his lecture entitled, "Pilgrim's Life," about his trip to the Holy Land. Virginia City was then in between its good years. April 27, Piper's Opera House was not full but Twain's lecture was much applauded.

July 6, 1868, Mark Twain again left California and returned to the East. Though he planned many times to visit the West, he never did.

In 1905, Robert Fulton, invited Mark Twain to Reno so that its citizens might honor him. Mark Twain was then seventy and unable to accept Fulton's invitation but he wrote Fulton a moving letter May 24, 1905:

Dear Mr. Fulton:

I remember, as if it were yesterday, that when I disembarked from the overland stage in front of the Ormsby in Carson City in August, 1861, I was not expecting to be asked to come again. I was tired, discouraged, white with alkali dust, and did not know anybody; and if you had said then, "Cheer up, desolate stranger, don't be downhearted--pass on, and come again in 1905," you cannot think how grateful I would have been and how gladly I would have closed the contract...

...I thank you sincerely for the invitation; and with you, all Reno, and if I were a few years younger, I would accept it, and promptly. I would go. I would let somebody else do the oration, but, as for me, I would talk--just talk--and have the time of my life! I would march the unforgotton and unforgettable antiques by, and name their names, and give them reverent "Hail-and-farewell" as they passed:

Goodman, McCarthy Gillis, Curry, Baldwin, Winters, Howard, Nye, Stewart, Neely Johnson, Hal Clayton, North, Root, and my brother--upon whom be peace!--and then the desperados, who made life a joy and the "Slaughterhouse" a precious possession: Sam Brown, Farmer Pete, Bill Mayfield, Six-fingered Jake, Jack Williams, and the rest of the crimson discipleship...Believe me, I would start a resurrection it would do you more good to look at than the next one will...

Those were the days!--those old ones. They will come no more. Youth will come no more. They were so full to the brim with the wine of life; there have been no others like them. It chokes me up to think of them. Would you like me to come out there and cry? It would not besteem my white head.

Goodbye. I drink to you all. Have a good time--and take an old man's blessing.

Mark Twain

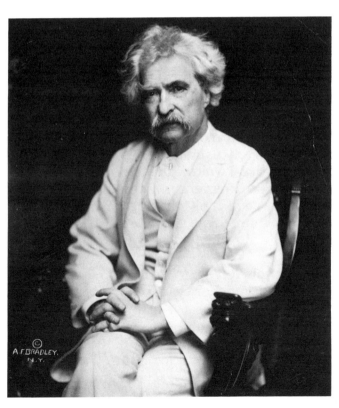

Mark Twain not long before his death. *Nevada Historical Society..*

EPILOGUE

Some events in our lives we take for granted but when looking back we discover they were turning points. Sam Clemens' matter-of-fact decision to accept a reporting post on the *Territorial Enterprise* was perhaps the most important decision he ever made but he was unaware of it at the time. For it was while reporting for the *Enterprise* that Clemens decided on writing as his profession and American literature was permanently changed. Mark Twain's eventual success as author, lecturer and celebrity stemmed from his twenty-one months on the *Enterprise*.

Mark Twain's talent as a humorist and writer was discovered by Joe Goodman. Twain was fortunate to work for this unusual editor, who allowed him to freely express himself in the columns of the *Enterprise*. Perhaps no other paper would have permitted Mark Twain as much freedom of expression as did the *Enterprise*. The *Enterprise* was the perfect place for Mark Twain to begin his serious writing career. The men of the *Enterprise* perfect in their support of Mark Twain's writing and development.

Walking away from Virginia City, Mark Twain took with him the mining camp's unpretentiousness, its humor, integrity, and its independent Western spirit. These he incorporated in his first successful books.

Mark Twain's apprenticeship on the *Enterprise* led to the publication of articles in the *Golden Era*, *The Californian* and other West Coast newspapers and to a reporting job on the San Francisco *Call* where Mark Twain's exposure of police corruption widened his notoriety. His trip to the Holy Land in 1867 as a correspondent for the *Alta California* provided Twain with material for his first book, *The Innocents Abroad*. His experiences as a miner and reporter in Nevada and California gave him material for his second book, *Roughing It*. These were immediate critical and financial successes and launched Mark Twain's long career as America's foremost author and humorist.

By the time Mark Twain left the West for good in 1868, he was the most popular humorist on the West Coast. This he accomplished in a matter of six years.

Mark Twain is endearing to Americans not only for his humor and stories but because his character and work reflect the independent, entrepreneurial spirit of America. Mark Twain was enormously gifted but talent alone did not account for his success. He possessed other skills and abilities coupled with his literary talent which made him successful.

Twain possessed that rare balance of creative talent and practical mindedness. As Joe Goodman noted, Mark Twain had the ability to market his talent. Mark Twain possesed extraordinary ambition and the willingness to sell himself and this opened many doors. Success didn't just happen for him. He worked hard at improving his writing craft and hard at promoting himself. While reporting for the *Enterprise* Mark Twain acquired work as a correspondent for the San Francisco *Call* which helped establish his reputation in the West. He sought publication for his writing in other Western journals. It was he who rented a hall in San Francisco, printed advertisments and launched his successful lecturing career. It was he who negotiated with the *Alta California* and persuaded the owners to subsidize his trip to the Holy Land which provided material for his first book. When the *Alta* refused to relinquish rights to the letters, it was Mark Twain who traveled all the way back to California to secure them. Mark Twain took full responsiblity for his life and career.

At bottom, Mark Twain worked hard and through his labors and aggressiveness became successful. He was like many great men of the nineteenth century, a self-made man. As a silver miner, as a reporter, as a lecturer, as a businessman, Mark Twain was willing to give all of himself for the long shot: he was willing to take a risk.

Though Mark Twain began his writing career fairly late, he was twenty-six, he did not view this as a barrier. He went forward with energy and enthusiasm. His social skills were a great aid. He had knocked around the world and had acquired a worldy knowledge and wisdom. He had met all types of people and was able to speak in a common language all understood. He was gregarious, fun to be with. He knew how to cultivate men of influence but did not do so solely for the sake of success. He liked being around successful men and these men in turn greatly influenced and inspired him.

In spite of his moodiness, bad temper and arrogance, he won friends and was a friend. When he became successful, he helped Dan De Quill launch his first book. Years later, when he learned Steve Gillis did not have a collection of his published works, Mark Twain saw that Gillis was sent a fine, leather bound collection. His homes were always open to his friends; Joe Goodman made several trips to the East to visit. Mark Twain made new friends but he did not forget old ones.

Most importantly, for all his self-debasement, Mark Twain was honest, dealt fairly with others; when he did wrong, he apologized; he was a man of integrity, highly moral. He cared deeply for the needs and sufferings of others. For all his joking about God and religious matters, though he considered himself a poor example, his actions showed him to be a responsible Christian, self-less and empathetic, though certainly not perfect. His temper did not mellow with age and he carried grudges with him to the grave. He had shortcomings but he made use of them by making fun of them in print and on the stage thus endearing himself to readers and audiences.

Virginia City, that gorgeous, spirited mining town where Mark Twain began his writing career, is still here. I encourage you to make a visit and discover for yourself the place where "Mark Twain" was born. Words cannot fully convey the experience of Virginia City. Come here and walk the streets where young Mark Twain walked; see the *Territorial Enterprise* building where Mark Twain wrote and got himself into trouble; view the mountains and the glorious sky that inspired him; come feel the force of the Washoe Zephyrs, see the mountains of rock and sand the miners dug out of the earth. Stop in the saloons for the excitement of slot machines, the world's biggeset hot dogs and cold drinks to soothe the summer's heat.

And if the Almighty grants me a long life, one summer's day we may meet in the Union Brewery Saloon on C Street and we'll talk and imagine together the life Mark Twain, Dan De Quille, Joe Goodman, Dennis McCarthey and others lived here when the mills pounded rocks into silver, the streets were paved with gold, the steam whistles screamed, when Mike the man-eater searched the saloon for his next nose to munch, and millions of dollars poured out of Virginia City and into the world.

And if you will stay a little while, maybe you will meet that glorious Nevada spirit, first brought to Virginia City by the romantic, adventurous young men--Mark Twain among them--still roaming the historic streets looking for a friendly face.

ACKNOWLEDGEMENTS

This book could not have been written without the assistance of a number of helpful persons and institutions.

As always, I thank my wife Edie, for her love, encouragement and support. She has given of herself unselfishly during the last ten years of this author's career.

Judy Craig, graphoanalyst, gave freely of her time and knowledge. Judy's graphoanalysis of Mark Twain's handwriting gave special insight to his mind and character.

Larry Tanner, President of the Storey County Historical Society, spent a couple of days with me romping around the hills of Virginia City and the streets of Carson City taking photographs for this book. Thanks Larry.

I thank Walt Daniels for his jeep tour of Six and Seven Mile canyons and for sharing his historical knowledge.

Richard Bendix provided photographic assistance.

The staff of the Mark Twain Project, University of California, Berkeley, supplied copies of Mark Twain's letters and photos and were a very big help.

Again, a special thanks to Phil Earl and Eric Moody of the Nevada Historical Society, living archives who patiently helped locate historical photos and material.

I owe a special thanks to the Mark Twain scholars who first uncovered details of the author's life in Nevada and California: Effie Mona Mack, Paul Fatout, Henry Nash Smith, and Ivan Benson.

Last, but always first, I thank you Lord, Jesus Christ, for your help with this book, for my wife and children, for my work and for the life you have given me here on your earth.

MARK TWAIN'S NEVADA YEARS AND LATER SUCCESS

July 26, 1861 - Sam Clemens, at twenty-five, leaves St. Joseph, Missouri by Overland Stage with his older brother, Orion, recently appointed Secretary of Nevada Territory.

August 14 - Arrives noon at Carson City, Nevada Territory. Rooms with Orion at a boarding house across from the plaza.

Late August - Makes first trip to Lake Tahoe with John Kinney.

Early September - Makes second trip to Lake Tahoe with Tom Nye. Stays three weeks and claims 300 acres of timber. "House" burns down and returns to Carson City.

October 26 - Writes first of several letters published in the Keokuk, Iowa *Gate City*.

November 30 - Turns twenty-six.

December 8-16 - During this week Sam, Billy Claggett, Jack Simmons and Mr. Tillou leave for Unionville, a silver mining camp 200 miles northeast of Carson City.

December 8-16 - After a weary and cold journey, Sam and his friends arrive at Unionville, build a crude shelter and begin prospecting.

Mid-January, 1862 - Discouraged with the poor prospects at Unionville, Sam returns to Carson City.

Early April - Takes one of the first stages to Aurora.

April 18 - Writes first letter to Orion from Aurora. Begins prospecting and mining with Horatio Phillips and Bob Howland.

May - Begins writing humorous "Josh" letters and sends them to the *Territorial Enterprise* at Virginia City, Nevada, then a booming mining town 15 miles from Carson City.

June 22 - Deeply involved with the Annipolitan claim; believes he and Orion will soon be millionaires.

July 30 - Receives offer from the *Enterprise* to become a reporter at $25 a week.

August 7 - Writes Orion that he has written Barstow of the *Enterprise* and accepted the reporting post.

August 8-15 - Makes a walking trip to the White Mountain Mining District, likely Long Valley, site of today's Crowley Lake, near Mammoth Lakes, California east of the Sierra Nevada mountains.

September 9 - Writes last letter from Aurora to Billy Claggett.

Mid-September - Arrives in Virginia City having walked 130 miles. Begins work on the *Enterprise* as a local reporter,

October 4 - Publishes first hoax, "Petrified Man".

Mid-November through December - In Carson City to report on the second Territorial Legislature.

January, 1863 - Back in Virginia City as local reporter.

January 31 - Sends dispatch from Carson City signed "Mark Twain", first time he has used pen name professionally though it appears others were calling him Mark before this dispatch.

Early May - Makes first trip to San Francisco with Clement T. Rice, the Unreliable, reporter for the Virginia City *Union*. Stays one month.

June - Returns to Virginia City.

July 26 - White House boarding house on C Street where Twain resides, burns down. Twain loses his clothing and some mining stock.

September 5 - Leaves for San Francisco.

Mid-October - Returns to Virginia City. Rooms with Dan De Quille who has recently returned from the East.

October 31 - Publishes the infamous "Massacre at Dutch Nick's."

November 1 - Admits horrible story was a hoax. Western newspaper editors are outraged. Twain offers to resign from the *Enterprise*.

November 2-December 11 - In Carson City to report on Constitutional Convention.

November 30 - Turns twenty-eight.

Early December - Returns to Virginia City for a special presentation when he is given a fake meerschaum pipe by *Enterprise* practical jokers.

About December 7 - Returns to Carson City.

December 23-29 - Humorist Artemus Ward in Virginia City for several lectures. Twain, Ward and *Enterprise* staffers go on one week binge.

January 12-February 20, 1864 - In Carson City to report on third Territorial Legislature. Elected "Governor" by Third House.

January 27 - Gives first public lecture at Carson City; attracts a large audience at a dollar a head. Donates money to the First Presbyterian Church of Carson City.

February 1 - Jennie Clemmens, Orion's only daughter dies of spotted fever.

February 7 - "Town Topics", New York *Sunday Mercury*.

February 21 - "Those Blasted Children", Twain's first story printed by an eastern publication in the New York *Sunday Mercury*.

Late February - Returns to Virginia City as local reporter.

February 27 - Adah Isaacs Menken, Famous actress and hopeful writer, arrives in Virginia City and seeks Twain's friendship.

March 6 - First issue of the Weekly Occidental, a literary journal, short lived, for which Twain, Tom Fitch and others were to collaborate.

April 1 - Twain publishes another hoax about rival editor and friend, Tom Fitch, "Another Traitor--Hang Him!"

May 16 - Ruel C. Gridley arrives in Virginia City selling the flour sack in efforts to collect money for the Sanitary Fund.

May 17 - Twain accuses Carson City ladies of diverting money from the Sanitary Fund to aid the Miscegenation Society.

May 24 - Twain denounces Laird of the Virginia *Union* for not accepting his challenge to duel.

May 29 - Following a warning from authorities that he would be arrested for demanding a duel, Twain and Steve Gillis leave Virginia City by stage for San Francisco.

June-December - Writes for the San Francisco *Morning Call*, denied a by-line and unable to contribute creative articles. Contributes creative articles to the *Golden Era* and the *Californian*, literary journals. Supplies the *Enterprise* with at least one dispatch.

December - Flees San Francisco with Steve Gillis for Jim Gillis' cabin on Jackass Hill near Sonora in the gold mining Mother Lode country. Departure is caused by Twain's exposure of San Francisco police corruption first published in the *Call* later in the *Enterprise*.

January-February, 1865 - Whiles his time away on Jackass Hill with Jim Gillis who becomes a lifetime friend. First hears the story of the Jumping Frog while at a hotel at nearby Angel's Camp. During this period Twain comes close to committing suicide.

October-March, 1866 - Contributes to the *Enterprise*, San Francisco and Sacramento newspapers to earn a living.

November 1865 - "Jumping Frog" appears in the New York *Saturday Press*. Story becomes an immense success and is reprinted in newspapers throughout America. Twain's first national recognition.

March 7, 1866 - Sails to the Sandwich (Hawaiian) Islands to write a series of articles for the Sacramento *Union*. Meets Anson Burlingame, U.S. Minister to China, who encourages Twain.

June 25 - Writes special dispatch about the burning clipper ship

Hornet and its survivors. *Hornet* articles help cement Twain's West Coast career.

October 2 - Rents hall at the San Francisco Academy of Music and presents his second paid lecture on the Sandwich Islands. Newspapers praise lecture. Twain decides to take lecture to the mining camps of northern California and northwestern Nevada. Tour is great success.

October 27 - Arrives in Virginia City for lecture on October 31. Piper's Opera House on B Street crammed; hour and a half lecture brings the house down. Lectures at Dayton Nov. 7, Silver City Nov. 9, and Gold Hill Nov. 10.

December 13 - Leaves California for New York by ship.

May 1867 - *The Celebrated Jumping Frog of Calaveras County* and Other Sketches, published by C.H. Webb, New York.

May 6 - First New York lecture at Cooper Union a great success. Helps establish Twain's reputation on the East Coast.

June 8 - **Sails on the** *Quaker City* for the Holy Land as a correspondent for the San Francisco *Alta California*.

November 19 - Returns to New York. Moves to Washington, D.C. where he serves briefly as secretary to Senator William Stewart of Nevada. Stewart allows Twain to live at his house while writing, *The Innocents Abroad*, Twain's first book based on articles he wrote for the *Alta California*.

March 1868 - Returns to California in order to secure rights to letters written for the *Alta California*.

April 24 - Arrives in Virginia City to present his "Sandwich Island," lecture.

July 6 - Leaves California for good.

1869 - *The Innocents Abroad* published; becomes an immediate success.

February 2, 1870 - At thirty-five, marries Olivia Langdon.

February 1872 - *Roughing It* published.

December 1873 - *The Guilded Age* published.

July 21, 1875 - *Sketches, New and Old*.

December 1876 - *The Adventures of Tom Sawyer*.

March 1880 - *A Tramp Abroad*.

January 1882 - *The Prince and the Pauper*.

May 1883 - *Life on the Mississippi*.

January 1885 - *Adventures of Huckleberry Finn*.

December 1889 - *A Connecticut Yankee in King Arthur's Court*.

May 1896 - *Personal Recollections of Joan of Arc.*
June 1900 - *The Man That Corrupted Hadleyburg and Other Stories.*
April 1904 - *Extracts from Adam's Diary.*
June 5, 1904 - Olivia Langdon Clemens dies.
April 21, 1910 - Mark Twain dies and is buried at Elmira, New York beside Olivia and his daughters, Susie and Jean.

BIBLIOGRAPHY

The following is a partial bibliography students and scholars may find useful.

Unpublished Sources:

The Mark Twain Papers, Mark Twain Project, University of California, Berkley

William Wright Correspondence, Bancroft Library, University of California, Berkley

Newapaper and Magazine Sources:

Territorial Enterprise
Gold Hill News
Virginia Daily Union
Virginia Evening Bulletin
Virginia Chronicle
San Francisco Call
San Francisco Bulletin
The Californian
The Golden Era
OLD PIUTE
Alta California
Sacramento Union
California Illustrated Magazine
Nevada Magazine

Books:
Benson, Ivan: *Mark Twain's Western Years,* Russell and Russell, 1938.

Brand, Edgar Marquis: *The Literary Apprenticeship of Mark Twain,* University of Illinois Press, 1958.

Browne, Lena F.: *J. Ross Browne: His Letters, Journals and Writing,* University of New Mexico Press, 1969.

Clemens, Clara: *My Father Mark Twain,* Harper and Bros., 1931.

De Quille, Dan: *The Big Bonanza,* Alfred Knopf, 1947.

De Quille, Dan: *"Reporting With Mark Twain,"* California Illustrated Magazine, Vol. IV, 1893.

De Quille, Dan: "Artemus Ward In Nevada," California Illustrated Magazine, August, 1893.

DeVoto, Bernard: *Mark Twain's America,* Houghton Mifflin Company, 1932.

Doten, Alfred: *The Journals of Alfred Doten,* edited by Walter Van Tilburg Clark, University of Nevada Press, 1973. *"Early Journalism in Nevada,* The Nevada Magazine, Vol. I, No. 3, 1899.

Fatout, Paul: *Mark Twain in Virginia City,* Indiana University Press, 1964.

Frady, Steven R.: *Red Shirts and Leather Helmets,* University of Nevada Press, 1984.

Gillis, William: *Memories of Mark Twain and Steve Gillis,* The Banner, 1924.

Howells, W.D.: *My Mark Twain,* Harper and Bros., 1911.

Goodwin, Charles C.: *As I Remember Them,* Salt Lake Commercial Club, 1913.

Kelly, J. Wells: *First Directory of Nevada Territory,* San Francisco, 1862. *Second Directory of Nevada Territory,* 1863,

Lewis, Oscar: *Silver Kings,* Alfred Knopf, 1947.

Long, E. Hudson: *Mark Twain Handbook,* Hendricks House, 1957.

Mack, Effie Mona: *Mark Twain in Nevada,* Charles Scribner's Sons, 1947.

Moody, Eric: *Western Carpetbagger,* University of Nevada Press, 1978.

Paine, Albert Bigelow: *Mark Twain: A Biography,* Harper and Bros., 1912. *Mark Twain's Letters, Vol. I,* Harper and Bros., 1917

Rogers, Franklin: *The Pattern For Mark Twain's Roughing It,* University of California Press, 1961.

Smith, Henry Nash and Anderson, Frederick: *Mark Twain Of The Enterprise,* University of California Press, 1957.

Stewart, William M.: *Reminiscences,* Neale Publishing Co., 1908.

Twain, Mark: *The Autobiography of Mark Twain,* Edited by Charles Neider, Harper and Row, 1959; *"Curing A Cold"; Life on the Mississippi; "My Bloody Massacre"; "My Late Senatorial Secretaryship"; Roughing It; Sketches New and Old; The Innocents Abroad.*

Weisenberger, Francis Phelps: *Idol of The West,* Syracuse University Press, 1965.

INDEX

Order these great books by mail today
Autographed and inscribed by George Williams III.
Or call 1-800-487-6610 for a Free brochure

NEW! In the Last of the Wild West. The true story of the author's attempt to expose the murders of prostitutes and corruption in Virginia City, Storey County, Nevada, home of the largest legal brothel in the United States. 272 pages. AUTOGRAPHED. $12.95 quality paperback; $24.95 hard cover.

ROSA MAY: THE SEARCH FOR A MINING CAMP LEGEND Virginia city, Carson City and Bodie, California were towns Rosa May worked as a prostitute and madam 1873-1912. Read her remarkable true story based on 3 1/2 years of research. Praised by the *Los Angeles Times* and *Las Vegas Review Journal*. Includes 30 rare photos, 26 personal letters. 240 pages. AUTOGRAPHED. $10.95 quality paperback; hard cover, $16.95. Soon to be a television movie.

THE REDLIGHT LADIES OF VIRGINIA CITY, NEVADA Virginia City was the richest mining camp in the American West. The silver from its mines built San Francisco and helped the Union win the Civil War. From 1860-95, Virginia City had three of the largest redlight districts in America. Here women from around the world worked the world's oldest profession. Author Williams tells the stories of the strange lives of the redlight girls, their legends and violent deaths. Based on newspaper accounts, county records and U.S. Census information. Perhaps the best and most informative book on prostitution in the old West. Plenty of historic photos, illustrations, map and letters. 48 pages. AUTOGRAPHED. $5.95 quality paperback; hard cover, $10.95.

2nd revised edition HOT SPRINGS OF THE EASTERN SIERRA Here are more than 40 natural hot spring pools author George Williams III has located from the Owens Valley, through the Eastern Sierra recreation corridor to Gerlach, Nevada. George has tracked down every hot spring worth "soaking" in. Included are many secret springs only known to locals. George gives easy to follow road directions, and his "2 cents" about each spring are informative and entertaining. Maps by the author help you find these secret springs easily. 72 pages. AUTOGRAPHED. $7.95 quality paperback; hard cover, $12.95.

THE GUIDE TO BODIE AND EASTERN SIERRA HISTORIC SITES True story of the rise and fall of Bodie, California's most famous mining camp, today a ghost town, National Historic Site and California State Park. Known as the toughest gold mining town in the West where millions were made in a few years, murders were a daily occurrence. Has a beautiful full color cover with 100 photos on an 8 1/2 X 11 format. 88 pages. AUTOGRAPHED. $10.95 quality paperback; hard cover, $16.95.

THE MURDERS AT CONVICT LAKE True story of the infamous 1871 Nevada State Penitentiary break in which 29 outlaws escaped and fled more than 250 miles into Mono and Inyo counties, California. They vowed to kill anyone who got in their way. In a terrible shootout at Monte Diablo, today known as Convict Lake just south of Mammoth Lakes ski resort, the convicts killed two men. They fled to nearby Bishop where they were captured and hanged. Includes 18 rare photographs and pen and ink drawings by Dave Comstock. 32 pages. AUTOGRAPHED. $4.95 quality paperback; hard cover, $12.95.

MARK TWAIN: HIS ADVENTURES AT AURORA AND MONO LAKE When Sam Clemens arrived in Nevada in 1861, he wanted to get rich quick. He tried silver mining at Aurora, Nevada near Mono Lake not far from Yosemite National Park. Clemens didn't strike it rich but his hard luck mining days led to his literary career. 32 rare photos, mining deeds and maps to places where Clemens lived, wrote and camped. 100 pages. AUTOGRAPHED. $6.95 quality paperback; hard cover, $12.95.

NEW! MARK TWAIN: HIS LIFE IN VIRGINIA CITY, NEVADA While reporting for the *Territorial Enterprise* in Virginia City, 1862-64, Sam Clemens adopted his well known pen name, Mark Twain. Here is the lively account of Mark Twain's early writing days in the most exciting town in the West. Over 60 rare photos and maps to places Twain lived and wrote. 208 pages. AUTOGRAPHED. $10.95 paperback; hard cover, $24.95.

Mark Twain: Jackass Hill and the Jumping Frog by George Williams III. The true story of Twain's discovery of "The Celebrated Jumping Frog of Calaveras County," the publication of which launched his international career. After getting run out of Virginia City, Twain settled in San Francisco in May, 1864. He went to work as a common reporter for the San Francisco *Call*. After five frustrating months, Twain quit the *Call* and began hanging around with Bret Harte, then editor of the popular *Golden Era*, a West Coast magazine. When Twain posted bail for a friend and the friend skipped town, Twain followed and headed for Jackass Hill in the foothills of the Sierra Nevada near Sonora.There Twain lived with his prospector friend Jim Gillis in a one room log cabin on Jackass Hill. After a discouraging prospecting trip, in a saloon at Angel's Camp, Twain was told the Jumping Frog story by a bartender. Twain's version, published eleven months later, became an international hit. "The Celebrated Jumping Frog of Calaveras County," is included in this book.
116 pages, index, bibliography, 35 historic photographs, guide maps for travelers. AUTOGRAPHED. Quality paper $6.95; hard cover $12.95

New for Spring 1993! On the Road with Mark Twain in California and Nevada
Here is a handy, easy to read guide to Mark Twain's haunts in California and
Nevada 1861-68. Has road directions to historic sites, guide maps and lots of
photographs of Twain, the historic sites and Twain's friends. Gives brief run-
downs of each place and tells what Twain was doing while there. A must-have
book for any Twain fan who would like to follow his trail in the far West. 150
pages, many photos, road maps, index. $12.95 quality paper; $24.95 hard cover.

Order Form

To order books **Toll Free** with *VISA* or MasterCard call **1-800-487-6610**, 9 AM to
5 PM West Coast time Monday through Friday. **Phone orders are shipped the
same day received. Call for a Free brochure.**

Name _____
Address_____City_____
State_____Zip_____

Yes, George send me the following books, autographed and inscribed:
___Copy(ies) In the Last of the Wild West, 12.95 pap.; 24.95 hard cover
___Copy(ies) Rosa May: The Search For A Mining Camp Legend, 9.95 pap.;
16.95 hard
___Copy(ies) The Redlight Ladies of Virginia City, 5.95 pap.; 10.95 hard cover
___Copy(ies) Hot Springs of the Eastern Sierra, 7.95 pap.; $12.95 hard cover
___Copy(ies) The Guide to Bodie, 10.95 pap.; 16.95 hard cover
___Copy(ies) The Murders at Convict Lake, 4.95 pap.; 12.95 hard cover
___Copy(ies) Mark Twain: His Adventures at Aurora, 6.95 pap.; 12.95 hard
cover
___Copy(ies) Mark Twain: His Life In Virginia City, Nevada, 10.95 pap.; 24.95
hard
___Copy(ies) Mark Twain: Jackass Hill and the Jumping Frog, $6.95 pap.; 12.95
hard cover
___Copy(ies) On the Road with Mark Twain In California and Nevada, 12.95
pap.; 24.95 hard cover
Shipping by postal service is 1.75 for the first book, .75 each additional book.
Faster shipping via UPS is 3.00 for the first book. 1.00 each additional book.

Total for books_____
Shipping   _____
Total enclosed in check or money order _____
Mail your order to:

Tree By The River Publishing
PO Box 935-MTVC
Dayton, Nevada 89403